Madame Alexander Dolls

An American Legend

Madame Alexander Dolls
An American Legend

Photography by Walter Pfeiffer

Text by Stephanie Finnegan

Contributing Expert, Historical Dolls: Lia Sargent

Additional Consultants
Pat Burns
A. Glenn Mandeville
Benita Schwartz

A Robert Campbell Rowe Book/Portfolio Press

On the cover is Karen Ballerina, 14 inches, hard plastic, 1947-48. On the back cover are Pearl of the Twenties, top, and Degas Ballerina. Each doll is 10 inches high, hard plastic, 1998. On the opposite page are two Alexanderkins ballerinas, each 8 inches, hard plastic, 1953.

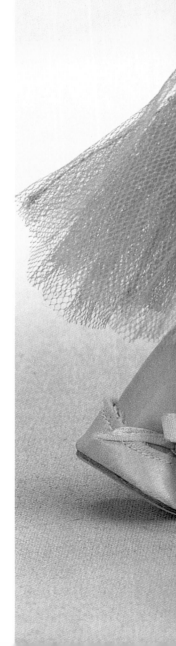

First Edition/First Printing

Copyright 1999 © Alexander Doll Company, Inc. and Portfolio Press Corporation

All rights reserved. No part of the contents of this book may be reproduced without the written permission of the publisher.

Library of Congress Catalog Card Number 98-67943

ISBN 0-942620-22-4

Project Editor: Krystyna Poray Goddu

Designed by John Vanden-Heuvel Design

Printed and bound by Milanostampa S.P.A., Turin, Italy

Contents

Part 1

The Madame:

Her Life and Her Company

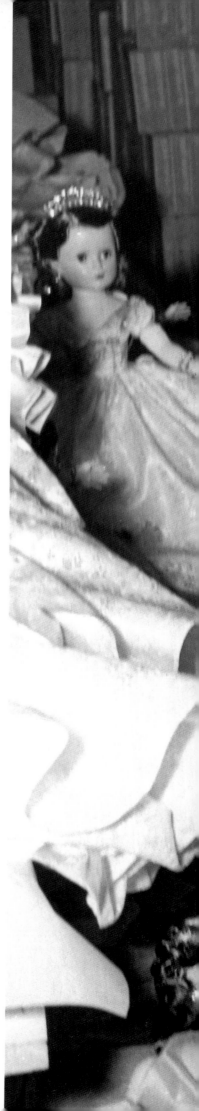

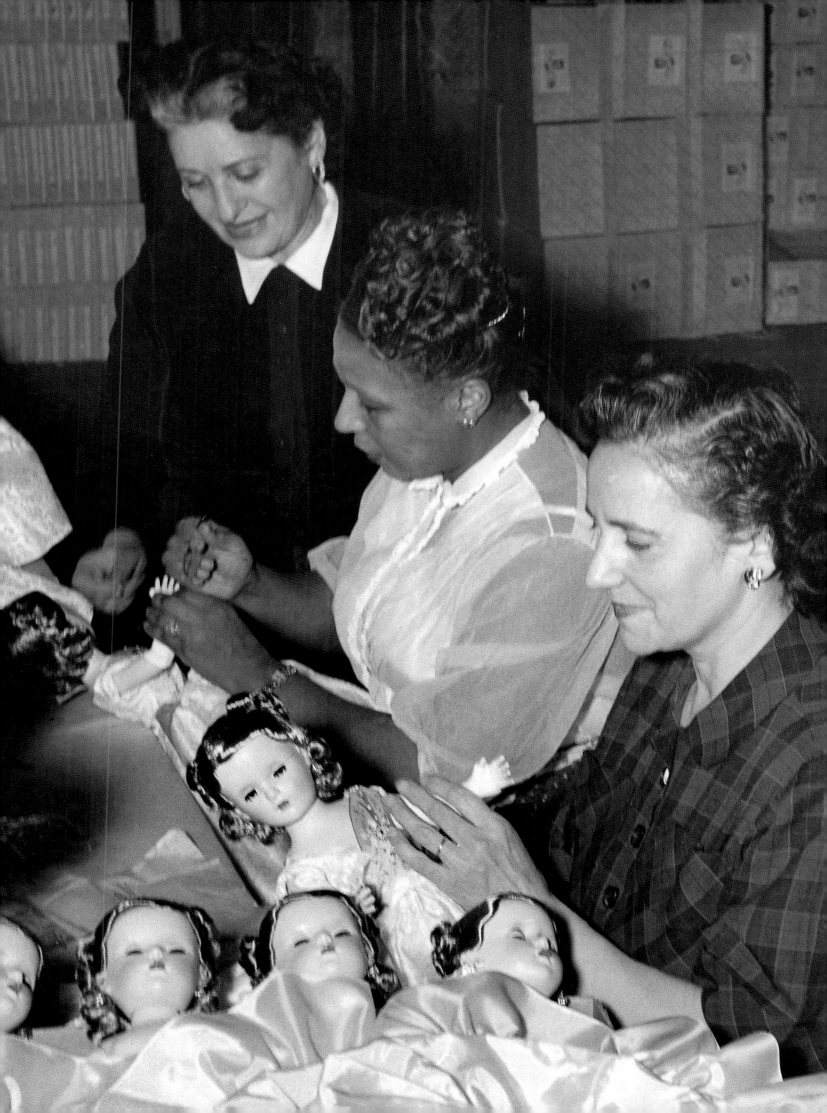

The Early Years

The dollmaker extraordinaire known as Madame Beatrice Alexander was born in the Williamsburg neighborhood of Brooklyn, New York, on March 9, 1895. At the time of her birth, the infant was known as Bertha, but when she grew older she changed her name to the more elegant Beatrice, manifesting her lifelong determination to better and romanticize herself. From early childhood, Beatrice constantly sought ways to express herself and to rise above the station to which she was born.

Beatrice's mother was Hannah Pepper, an Austrian-born immigrant who arrived in America by way of Russia. Like many Russian émigrés of the late-nineteenth century, Hannah had been a victim of the Russian pogroms—cruel and vicious attacks against Jewish citizens orchestrated by the nation's leader, Czar Alexander III, and his tutor, Konstantin Pobyedonostzev. The army of Cossacks that carried out this state-ordained reign of terror was monstrous in its persecution of Jewish men, women and children. As a result of their unstoppable rampage of rape, murder and pillage, more than two million Yiddish-speaking Eastern Europeans fled to the United States between 1881 and 1920. Among the refugees who found themselves packed daily onto steamer ships, where they endured squalid, depersonalized steerage-class conditions, was young Hannah.

For decades, the tale surrounding Beatrice's birth told of Hannah arriving in her new homeland, meeting and then marrying Maurice Alexander, a fellow immigrant who fathers Beatrice and three more daughters. However, according to some family members, this is not accurate. Beatrice retold the story of her parents' meeting so many times that even her own descendants are not quite sure what actually transpired. The only fact that the family is certain of is that Maurice Alexander was not Beatrice's biological father. One family-told tale relates that Hannah's husband died during a pogrom in Russia, along with their young children. Hannah, pregnant with Beatrice, managed to escape to freedom, and America. Another variation depicts Hannah and her Russian husband arriving together in the United States and settling in New York City, where she gives birth to her first daughter.

Top: This handpainted miniature of young Beatrice is the only known photograph of her as a child. Opposite page: Four generations of Alexander women are captured in this circa-1930s photo. From left: Mildred Behrman Birnbaum, Wendy Ann Birnbaum, Hannah Pepper Alexander, Beatrice Alexander Behrman.

Their seemingly happy future is abruptly cut short when her husband unexpectedly passes away, leaving Hannah widowed, with a seventeen-month-old child. Whichever origin is correct, one consistent thread does emerge. Beatrice Alexander was so enamored of her stepfather, Maurice, that she did everything in her power when recounting her family life to make him her one true father.

"They were two peas in a pod," Kathleen Blotney Birnbaum, Madame Alexander's granddaughter-in-law, states. "Granny just loved Maurice. He was the only father she had ever known. And they shared so much. They had their love of dollmaking and doll repairing in common. She took to that, whereas her three younger sisters really didn't."

Had Maurice Alexander not befriended and betrothed Hannah Pepper, would Beatrice have grown up to be the dynamic force she was in the doll industry? Bright, willful, talented and gifted—she seemingly would have risen to the top of whatever career she selected. However, Maurice's founding of America's first doll hospital certainly helped to steer her onto the path of children and their playthings. The doll hospital was located on Grand Street on New York City's Lower East Side. The Alexander family, which eventually numbered six, lived above the busy shop. Prior to his arrival in America, Maurice, who was born in Odessa, Russia, but moved to Germany as a young man, had apprenticed to a gentleman who repaired mechanical toys, clocks and china. A skillful craftsman with a knack for repairing watches and other fine trinkets, Maurice quickly learned the art of restoring fragile porcelain dolls. More important, he developed an instinct for knowing why dolls were so pleasing to little girls and their doting parents. Maurice's business was also soon given a boost by an association he had struck up with Robert Foulds, a Scotsman who had inherited a dry-goods/toy business. Clients who bought from Foulds were often referred to the able hands of Maurice Alexander, if and when tragedy befell their German china-heads or their French bisque babies.

According to relatives, historians and collectors, the doors to the Alexander Doll Hospital swung open in 1895, coincidentally the same year that Beatrice was born. The doll hospital was situated in the center of a teeming mecca for immigrants. The year 1896 saw the birth of Henry Ford's first automobile, but the streets of Beatrice's neighborhood were overflowing with horses and wagons, pushcarts, itinerant tinkers and throngs of pedestrians. Nary an expensive horseless carriage was in sight. Conversations in Yiddish, German, Russian, Romanian and Polish cascaded across alleyways and street corners. Grandfathers and grandmothers, mothers and fathers spoke comfortably with one another in the native tongues of lands left behind. But the children! Oh, the children were an entirely different story. The grandparents and parents were determined to make sure that their youngsters excelled in every way. America was not like other countries where a pecking order was assigned at birth. These folks remembered sailing into New York Harbor, standing on the ships' decks, nudging one another and pointing at the Statue of Liberty. Many of them were aware that the philosophy of this nation—"Give me your tired, your poor, your huddled masses yearning to breathe free"—was written by Emma Lazarus, an American Jewish woman, in her 1882 poem, "The New Colossus." Surely, these were friendly shores!

Hannah and Maurice Alexander felt that same limitless optimism, and they encouraged their daughters, Beatrice, Rose, Florence and Jean, to study hard and to strive for all that they could. "The neighborhood was a tough one," Mildred Behrman Birnbaum, Madame Alexander's daughter, reminisces. "It was a ghetto, where people lived on top of one another. People were poor, but what little they had, they were always willing to share. They hoped and prayed that they would each have a little bit of success."

Beatrice took these good wishes seriously. She excelled at school and won many top honors during her academic career. When she was finished with her household chores, she would retreat to a space behind the family doll shop and hospital, an area that she had begged her parents to convert into a secret garden.

There, surrounded by roses, tulips and daisies that defied the cement and broken pavement, she lost herself in the poetry of Keats, Tennyson, Longfellow and Fields. She devoured the novels of Dickens, Carroll and Alcott. *Little Women*, authored by Louisa May Alcott, chronicled the adventures of the four March sisters and their devotion to family and friends. This wholesome look at Civil War fortitude and strong family values was especially important to Beatrice. The March girls' fictional lives of good works and good intentions colored her real-life upbringing, and proba-

The doors to the Alexander Doll Hospital swung open in 1895, coincidentally the same year that Beatrice was born.

bly played a strong hand in her eventual growth into a world-famous businesswoman.

As Beatrice flipped the pages of Alcott's ruminations on levelheaded Meg, feisty, sharp-tongued Jo, sensitive, musical Beth and artistic, flirtatious Amy, was she aware that one day she would incorporate the personality traits of all four heroines into the flamboyant persona that the world would come to know and love as Madame Alexander? Did she envision that she would create cloth replicas of these valiant young women in 1930, and that sixty-eight years later, Little Women dolls would continue to be made bearing her name? It is unlikely that Beatrice would have spun such accurate, prescient fantasies, but she certainly dreamed big dreams. Lia Sargent, a well-known dealer of vintage Alexander dolls, and a friend of Madame's toward the end of the dollmaker's life, recalls Madame telling her, "There are rich people in life, and there are poor people in life. I'd rather throw my lot in with the rich." Sargent laughs when she imparts this remembered quote because it was "delivered without any apology.

She didn't need to make an excuse for her feelings. She didn't apologize for wanting to have more than she was born with. It was how she felt and she wasn't ashamed. And let's be honest, why should she have been?"

In countless magazine articles, Beatrice informed her interviewers that she was deeply influenced by the wealthy carriage trade that frequented her father's business. She spoke evocatively and emotionally to Lia Sargent of the "grand ladies sweeping up to our house, riding in carriages and wearing ostrich-feathered hats. I vowed that someday I would have a carriage and I would have those feathers!"

Indeed, Beatrice Alexander would come one day to surround herself with the best that money could buy. She filled several homes with rare possessions and brilliant works of art. And she made sure that this devotion to fine, exquisite detailing carried over to her dollmaking business, as well. It is easy to see how the little girl with the long, brown sausage curls and the big brown eyes would mentally record the comings and goings of these New York swells. Storing away the details of their velvet waistcoats, fringed reticules, laced-up leather boots and dainty parasols, she committed their Edwardian finery to the recesses of her active mind. She would eventually draw upon her memories of their fashionable attire just as she would draw upon her own inner strength.

In 1912, when Beatrice was seventeen, she graduated from Washington Irving High School. She was her class valedictorian and was honored with a complete set of Shakespeare's plays in recognition of her artwork. Her artistic tendencies must have been constantly on display during her years at Washington Irving. In a May 14, 1967, interview with the *Washington Post*, she told a reporter that at age sixteen she had won a scholarship to study sculpting in Paris. Unfortunately, her parents did not grant her permission to go overseas. The bank where they had carefully and faithfully deposited their weekly income over the years had faltered; their life-savings was lost.

Madame's husband, Philip Behrman, was an integral part of the Alexander Doll Company, handling many of the difficult decisions with his wife until his death in 1966.

It is understandable why Maurice and Hannah chose to keep their daughter close to home, but this taste of financial ruination left a bitter, lingering flavor in Beatrice's mouth. Loss of money prevented her from traveling to Paris, stopped her from becoming a sculptress, barred her from entering the grand salons along the Seine. Though she was forced to abandon her dream of Paris and to remain on New York's Lower East Side, she made up her mind that her tenure as a regular, everyday, working-class clerk would not last long.

Beatrice Alexander followed the conservative traditions of her day and married Philip Behrman on June 30, 1912, a few weeks after graduation. Philip was employed in the personnel department of a local hat factory, and there was genuine love and appreciation between the young newlyweds. Beatrice praised her spouse and business partner in a 1977 Palm Beach lifestyle newspaper. The article, tailored for Thanksgiving, concentrated on well-known Americans and what they were grateful for. Beatrice told the author, "No person is self-made. We know that behind every successful man there is a woman, and behind every successful woman there is a man. My man was Philip. Throughout my life, he shielded me from the

"I was able to become what I became because of Philip and his love and support of me," Madame once said.

ugly and unglamorous end of my business so I could be free to do the creative work. I was able to become what I did because of Philip and his love and support of me."

True to her pledge, Beatrice did not linger as a book-keeper at the Irving Hat Store, where she had been gainfully employed. It took an event of cataclysmic, civilization-quaking importance to free her from the ledger. Namely, it took World War I. Waged from 1914 to 1918, the Great War was the largest debacle of mass destruction that the world had witnessed to that time. One of the by-products of the war was an American embargo against German goods, including the dolls that were a mainstay of the Alexander family's repair and retail business. This, too, had a devastating impact on Maurice and Hannah. What good was a doll shop if its shelves were bare and its windows empty? However, the four Alexander sisters, determined to succeed, did not allow their parents' pessimism to persist. (The exact dates for the following chain of events are subject to debate. For purposes of this narration, it has been decided to follow the records that pinpoint the breakthrough cloth dolls as being made during World War I.)

Goaded by the enthusiasm of their eldest sibling, Rose, Florence and Jean rolled up their sleeves and congregated around the family kitchen table. In a tableau of sisterly togetherness that would have made Miss Alcott proud, the four little Alexander women brainstormed on how to create a doll without benefit of kiln and porcelain. The girls took to this avocation with a vengeance. In a circa-1930 interview with the *World Telegram*, Beatrice told syndicated columnist Mary Margaret McBride, "My sisters and I all saw the first light of day in a room surrounded by the legs, arms and torsos of dolls awaiting repair. I do remember the fits and tears that children experienced when their porcelain dolls shattered. I made up my mind in my youth to make a doll that would be unbreakable." The scarcity of materials and this personal resolve led Beatrice to hit upon the idea of creating cloth playthings to sell in Maurice's shop. But cloth renderings of what exactly? The War was on everyone's mind, and Beatrice decided to salute the brave women who had risked their lives on the front. She conjured up a Red Cross Nurse doll, made from muslin and stuffed with excelsior. The dolls were an instant success, and Beatrice was flushed with the heady joy of creating something for which the public clamored.

During the war years, in 1915, Beatrice had given birth to her daughter, Mildred. She always considered Mildred to be her greatest creation. ("The happiest moment of my life?" Madame Alexander contemplated in a November 1988 *Dolls* magazine interview with Krystyna Poray Goddu. "When I opened my eyes and saw my baby next to me," she concluded.) Even though a child and a husband to care for kept the young woman quite busy and satisfied in one area of her life, her creative side was unleashed with the success of the Red Cross Nurse dolls. She hungered to be more than just a wife and a mother, and she found herself returning to the sewing circle that gathered regularly around her parents' kitchen table. There, Beatrice instructed her sisters in

Above: Madame and her young daughter, Mildred, posed for this photo circa 1920. Opposite page: In the early dollmaking days, Madame puts her careful attention to the creation of a head.

the production of well-crafted, swiftly made nurse dolls. She also tried her hand at sewing a cloth baby rag doll. She would make a doll sample, and then show it to her sisters and mother for comments. As her sisters copied her stitching and painting style, she would pace behind them, looking over their shoulders, offering encouragement or critiquing their work when it did not meet her standards. "That was my first training for becoming an executive," she later told her secretary, Frances ("Miss Frances") Einhorn. That personal, hands-on approach was the business style that Beatrice

maintained during her seventy-five-year dollmaking career.

"You never knew when she would suddenly get it into her head to take a walk on the factory floor," Miss Frances, who remained Madame's personal secretary for more than thirty years, confides. "Every day she would walk literally miles across the factory floor. I guess you could say she was conducting spot inspections. She demanded the best from everyone who worked beside her because she demanded the best of herself."

Grandson William Alexander Birnbaum, who grew up to work alongside his revered grandmother and grandfather at the doll company, echoes Miss Frances' sentiments. "Let me tell you, I had tough bosses," he recalls. "I might walk in at five after nine, and I'd say good morning. My grandfather would raise his eyebrows and look at his wristwatch. My grandmother was just as tough. She didn't want me to be treated with kid gloves because I was her grandson. She hired me to be a worker, and that's what she expected from me: work!"

Tales of Beatrice's acerbic and outspoken critiques abound. Admirers and friends are quick to point out that despite her feminine demeanor and courtly ways, Beatrice was apt to speak her mind, and wasn't always conscious of how harsh or cutting her opinions would sound. "She didn't do it to be mean," Miss Frances explains. "It's just that she viewed the world in a certain way and she worked hard to get her company to fit that vision. If she saw lace on a hem that seemed to be frayed or uneven, she would complain and demand that it be fixed immediately. It wasn't nit-picking; she was the quality control of the whole company," Miss Frances concludes.

"She saw herself as an original," Kathleen Blotney Birnbaum concurs. "She was a responsible businesswoman whose name was in the public eye every day. And because she had a company to supervise, she had to make tough decisions, and that meant she had to be tough occasionally. Granny was known to say that after she was gone, there would never be another Madame Alexander. And her husband, Philip, would agree and say, 'Beatrice, when the Lord made you, He broke the mold.' Behind them, you could hear the entire company sigh, 'Thank God.'"

These seeds of setting a high standard for others, and an even higher one for herself, were sown in the early days of the Grand Street sewing circle. Pacing back and forth in her parents' home, dreaming up ideas and then watching them blossom, fed the artistic flame that had never stopped burning in Beatrice's soul. True, the Lower East Side wasn't the Paris that she pined for, but the humble confines of her family's kitchen were proving to be the equivalent of any Left Bank garret. Beatrice Alexander Behrman was about to embark on the riskiest endeavor of her life. She was about to forge her own doll-manufacturing company.

Coming of Age

The year was 1923, and the notion of a woman starting her own business was nearly unheard of. The 19th Amendment to the Constitution guaranteeing women the right to vote was enacted in 1920, just three years earlier. Women in the workplace were rare figures; women sitting in the boardroom were just about nonexistent! When Beatrice, at the age of twenty-eight, decided to begin the Alexander Doll Company, it wasn't a grandiose notion of corporate offices, multi-storied factories or hundreds of employees. It was a desire to succeed at something she had proven to be inherently good at. The cloth nurses and baby dolls that had filled her father's shop were immensely popular; why not branch out and sell more dolls to more stores? With $1,600 in start-up money, Beatrice hired additional laborers and purchased better supplies. The workforce that she assembled around the trusty kitchen table was comprised of the Alexander sisters and neighborhood men and women who were looking to earn additional dollars. The group would work late into the night, transforming cloth, muslin, yarn and glue into adorable infants and heart-warming toddlers.

The long hours and the hard work soon reaped enough money that Beatrice was able to move her enterprise out of the family kitchen above the doll hospital. She rented a studio in downtown Manhattan for forty dollars per month, and she divided her time between conceiving doll ideas, sewing doll bodies and costumes, and developing shop accounts. There was no formal distribution system at this time, so storekeepers

This early publicity photo is one of the first to identify the young doll manufacturer as Madame Alexander.

would arrive at the studio's door, with baskets hung over their arms, prepared to battle and bargain over inventory supply and cost. Beatrice held her own against these men, making sure that she received a fair price for her creations. She did not want to be perceived as a pushover simply because she was a female. During these early encounters with retailers, wholesale suppliers and bank-loan officers, Beatrice Alexander Behrman learned how to utilize her feminine wiles for maximum results. Always known to be something of a flirt, the petite businesswoman would smile and laugh and charm her masculine counterparts.

From 1923 through 1930, Beatrice relied upon the faith of her family and friends to see her through the ups and downs inherent in all fledgling businesses. She experienced fleeting successes as well as many setbacks. Though the early flat-faced cloth dolls did sell, Beatrice was not completely satisfied. "The dolls were beautiful, but too stiff and pokey," she wrote in the September 1957 edition of *Current Biography*. She was determined to improve upon their one-dimensional facial features. She began to experiment with sculpting in fabric, rather than just painting or sewing on features. "I wet some buckram and stretched it over a bowl and pushed it and let it dry, until my dolls could have a proper face with a nose and cheeks and a mouth," she explained in a 1983 *Town & Country* interview. The new style of cloth facial features proved so popular that it continued to be an Alexander mainstay into the 1940s.

Daughter Mildred suggests that her mother's inspiration for this breakthrough design wasn't completely self-propelled. "Mother always liked the Lenci line of dolls, and I know she wanted to make similar ones. She liked their straight legs and their pressed-felt faces. She was hoping to make American dolls that would be regarded as just as beautiful and just as elegant." The Lenci dolls, created in Italy, had debuted in 1919. Lenci was an acronym for the Italian phrase, "Ludus est nobis constanter industria." (English translation: Play is our constant work.) Their creator was an innovative, industrious woman named Elena Scavini, who often went by the aristocratic pseudonym of Madame Lenci. The

A penciled note on the back of this photo from the Alexander Doll Company archives states: "Alexander first doll, made in 1924 and 1923." However, the Alice in Wonderland appears to be one of the 1930 versions with pressed-felt molded features.

Italian-based Scavini's pioneering efforts in a male-dominated world mirror those of New York City's Beatrice Alexander Behrman. Many of Beatrice's confidantes mention how much she admired the Italian woman's stamina. "Madame told me that she came up with the title of 'Madame' for herself because of Signora Scavini," Tanya McWhorter, a personal friend and past president of the Madame Alexander Doll Club, observes. "She felt that Madame Lenci received respect and special courtesies because of that title. That Old World deference definitely appealed to Madame."

"I think she was taken by the notion of European aristocracy," Lia Sargent corroborates. "The self-bestowed title implies mystery, elegance and royalty. It's how she wanted to live her life since she was a little girl. She was able to make that fantasy come true." Sargent also points out that the abbreviation of M. Alexander was a silent tribute to Maurice, the father who had made the whole enterprise possible. (The first recorded mention of Beatrice Alexander Behrman as Madame Alexander is in the 1928 edition of *Playthings* magazine. Some associates and confidantes, however, remember her adoption of the aristocratic title occurring in 1925 at the urging of an advertising executive!)

During this seven-year period, 1923 to 1930, her daughter, Mildred, was growing from an understanding third-grader to an artistically proficient young woman. "I was eight years old when the company was founded," Mildred recalls. "Looking back, I guess I was what you would call a lonely child. We lived in the Bronx and I was looked after by a woman named Gertrude. We had a lovely apartment

across the street from the Bronx park, but my mother was never home to enjoy it." Mildred occupied herself with painting and drawing, and this juvenile pastime blossomed into a career as she entered adulthood. (As she matured, Mildred became a fine artist in her own right. Her paintings, in fact, were singled out for accolades at many group shows. Her proud mother decorated her various homes with Mildred's renderings and always pointed them out to journalists and visitors.)

For the sake of her doll business, Beatrice sacrificed many pleasures of motherhood. "My aunts looked after me on Saturdays. They would take me to see plays and Broadway revues," Mildred remembers. "My mother was off on Sundays, but we didn't really share any special routines on that day. She was exhausted from working six days a week, and she would relax by reading. She loved to expand her mind, and she often read difficult books—philosophy or theology were favorites."

Dating from the 1920s, this publicity shot shows Madame considering two unidentified dolls.

It may seem a bit peculiar that a woman who was so involved in the realm of daughters and dolls would be seemingly distant from her own offspring. Especially when the very same woman had been quoted as saying in hundreds of press releases that "the tendency of a little girl to clasp a doll to her chest is part of the natural maternal instinct." Mildred is quick to explain that it never crossed her mother's mind that she was not always on hand to witness the little, everyday events. "She was determined to give me what she didn't have as a child. She never forgot that she was poor as a child, and she wanted so much more than that for herself and her children. Working around the clock was a way to ensure it. She also told me that she never wanted a husband who was just a 'worker.' She wanted a husband who was a boss, an executive. Her parents used to joke when she was a little girl that it would take three husbands to keep her in the style she desired."

Philip Behrman, in fact, was reluctantly transformed into that fantasy super-mate. Realizing that a manufacturing company could not be run successfully by a single pair of hands, Beatrice asked Philip at some point in the mid 1920s (recorded dates conflict as either 1925 or 1926) to resign from his position as the personnel manager at the hat company. At first, the notion of resigning from a solid, reliable weekly pay check to risk everything in an upstart business simply terrified him. Beatrice would not tolerate fear. She handed him an astounding ultimatum: Either you work with me, or you can leave me. "I meant it," she told numerous journalists. "It seemed to me I could always get another man."

Mildred, however, does not believe that threat was made in earnest. "This was just how she conducted herself," the doll impresario's daughter explains. "When I was growing up, I never thought anything scared her. She was fearless. But now as an adult, I realize she was cloaking a lot of her fears. She would never let on, though. She didn't want to seem weak."

Filled with bravado and bullish tenacity, Beatrice and Philip worked together to expand the Alexander Doll Company from a simple studio setting. Those early years were straining ones, and Philip handled the tough, brow-beating matters. He decided how to handle the notion of unions; he calculated the weekly payroll; he estimated how much stock needed to be made during the slow seasons to have sufficient merchandise for the holidays. He would often take his wife aside and whisper that they weren't going to make it. She wouldn't listen to his nay-saying.

During one of these difficult times, Beatrice became convinced that if only she could secure a loan, everything would work itself out. She would get up in the morning, scour her closet for her most fashionable, well-groomed attire and march into a loan executive's office to plead her case. "Often she would grab me by the hand

and make sure that I accompanied her," Mildred reminisces. "It was for sympathy, you know. It would pull on the heartstrings."

Grandson William Birnbaum has often heard these tales of the early jockeying with little Mildred in tow for loans and small-business advances. "It was a clever move," he acknowledges. "Here is this poor woman trying to start out on her own. She came across as struggling and needing help." The ploy worked. Beatrice was advanced a loan of five thousand dollars that secured her a storefront and factory space. At her ninetieth birthday celebration, held in Miami, Florida, Madame Alexander delighted a roomful of well-wishers with an anecdote about this first major loan. The banker who had granted her the money was invited to the dinner affair, and was formally introduced to the crowd. Madame Alexander told her spellbound audience that the banker did give her the loan, but didn't seem very optimistic. He seemed to regard her as a high risk, and she perceived that he honestly didn't expect her business to succeed. Not one to trifle with doubters, Beatrice swore to excel and to repay the loan before its due date. She accomplished this mission and never borrowed money from his institution again. The banker became a personal friend of Beatrice and Philip's, and Madame made sure that he always knew how magnificently her business was thriving. "I wanted to teach him a lesson," she asserted. "You need to believe in people's dreams, especially women's."

In the late 1920s, firmly ensconced in their new grander space, with the production of cloth dolls continuing, the husband-and-wife team decided to buy doll bodies made of a new composition material (a mixture of sawdust, resin and papier-mâché). If Beatrice was serious about her desire to create unbreakable dolls, composition was a grand alternative. Freed from having to design body patterns and supervise body stuffing, Beatrice played around with more elaborate costuming and more fanciful finishing touches for the composition models. In the midst of this expansion, a mishap of inadequate engineering tested Beatrice's resolve. One morning the Alexander family walked into the factory and discovered all of their inventory submerged in four feet of water. The water tower perched atop of the building had burst and flooded everything in the floors below. One can only imagine how Beatrice must have reacted as she watched the outpourings of her heart and mind float by. Baby dolls and nurses, classical characters and dapper Dans drifted by, facedown. It was nearly the last straw for Beatrice, who would never let on that she had occasionally contemplated throwing in the towel. She admitted in a 1983 interview concerning her nascent years in the business to sometimes feeling "desperate and discouraged. I wanted to run away, but by then, I had employees. I had sixteen people who depended on me."

Hannah Pepper, Beatrice's mother, who had shown her own iron will when she boarded an American-bound ship from Russia, would not let the flood get her down. "She waded in and began gathering up as many little dresses as she could," Mildred Birnbaum recalls. "She took them home, wrung them out and hung them everywhere to dry." Hannah decided to hold a "water sale." Everything was drastically marked down in price, and the company managed to earn just enough money to keep the business afloat.

As the company rolled into the 1930s, the Alexander sisters had more than just water damage to contend with. The stock market crash of October 29, 1929, had plunged the nation into an economic tailspin. The Great Depression was hallmarked by high unemployment (16 million people in a population of 123 million were jobless in the United States during 1933), failing banks, failing agricultural prices and failing businesses. When folks could hardly afford to put food on their dinner table, how could they be convinced to spend hard-found money on dolls and doll apparel? During this time, sisters Jean and Rose left the company. Florence, however, was still on hand, and had taken on the task of public relations. She attended the large toy fairs and other industry-related expositions. She and Beatrice made sure to always refer to their creations as "an origi-nal line of strikingly dressed dolls." According to a 1930 issue of *Toys and Novelties* magazine: "No two Alexander dolls were dressed alike; they wore the newest fashions, and had attractive blending of colors." Additionally, the Alexander sisters and their employees offered a line of doll clothing made to fit dolls of all sizes. (Florence's role in the organization would come to an end when she began to keep company with a successful, busy theatri-cal manager.)

Beatrice made a point of spending time with the

FAO Schwarz placed one of Beatrice's very first orders, and the line of dolls bearing her name continues to this day to be among the famous store's leading sellers.

buyers from Sears, FAO Schwarz, Marshall Field's, Macy's and Gimbel's. Department stores, as well as mom-and-pop shops, were affected by the Depression. Beatrice had a particularly close connection with exec-utives at FAO Schwarz. When she first pondered the leap into full-time dollmaking in 1923, she had person-ally called on the lead buyer at the posh New York toy store. According to some sources, she arrived at the store's doorstep armed with a primitive cloth version of her daughter, Mildred, inquiring if they would like to place an order. The lady and her wares were greeted enthusiastically, and a healthy mutual admiration soci-ety was forged on the spot. FAO Schwarz placed one of Beatrice's very first orders, and the line of dolls bearing her name continues to this day to be among the famous store's leading sellers.

As the 1930s stretched before her, Beatrice wondered

if she would be able to reproduce the success of the Red Cross dolls sold from her father's store. Those cloth creations represented a perfect marriage of time, place and opportunity. But impulse buys could be a thing of the past for hard-hit mothers and fathers. Long, careful consideration might have to preface every doll purchase from now on. What could she design that would demand to be bought?

As she had done so often in her childhood, Beatrice turned to her volumes of children's literature. But now she wasn't a dreamy-eyed adolescent mooning over mock turtles and drowsy dormice. She was a wife and a mother and a businesswoman, who was well aware that the Hoovervilles of shanty tents and "lost men" were dotting more and more of the nation's landscape. While rifling through memories of her beloved make-believe companions, inspiration hit. In August 1930 Beatrice obtained a trademark for a cloth Alice in Wonderland doll. Issued as trademark 304,488, the 16-inch all-cloth doll had pressed-felt, raised features and was hand-painted in oils. The basic appearance of the doll was attributed to the well-known John Tenniel black-and-white illustrations. The 1930 Alexander Alice in Wonderland doll exists in two different versions. One is done with the flat, polished-cotton, painted-on countenance, a tried and true interpretation that had served Madame well throughout the 1920s. The one that created the stir, though, was the "new and improved" technique, with its pressed-felt molded features.

With Alice's success, the characters that had kept Beatrice company during her childhood queued up to be given three-dimensional life. In many cases, there were no portraits or four-color guidelines for a Charles Dickens character or a Francis Hodgson Burnett dandy, so tireless Beatrice relied upon her always fertile imagination. Her years as a top-notch student paid off, too, because she knew the value of libraries and research. She ventured to the main Manhattan branch of the New York Public Library and began sketching from history books and magazines the outfits that actual people wore in the past. Her belief in painstaking authenticity is a legacy that is still handed down from generation to generation of wardrobe designers at the Alexander Doll Company.

In the early 1930s, Beatrice designed cloth versions of the four Little Women, utilizing her sculpted three-dimensional style. Well aware of the power of words, she bundled up these Civil War sisters and set up an appointment with the powerful syndicated columnist Mary Margaret McBride. McBride was enchanted by these inventive cloth dolls that went miles beyond the notion of a rag doll. She devoted a half-page to the feisty, diminutive designer. The article concludes with McBride's observation: "Not only does Madame Alexander put soles on her dolls but also puts souls into them." (This encounter between McBride and Madame has an apocryphal nature all its own. There are parallel accounts that set the meeting in 1925, and according to this version, Madame entered the columnist's office armed with an extremely rare, never photographed set of Little Women rag dolls, which elicited the same "soulful" remark.)

In 1931, still fueled by the grand reaction to Alice, Madame also began to manufacture costumes for little girls. Perhaps due to her love for fine fashion, perhaps due to her own childhood longings for luxurious clothing—whatever the reason, this flirtation with dressing "living dolls" would haunt Beatrice throughout her life. It was a side business that she felt compelled to dabble with, though she never committed to it with the same verve she saved for her play mannequins. In 1933, Alice was re-issued as trademark 334,921. This time, the cloth doll had a bona-fide Hollywood affiliation. Paramount Pictures released in that year an all-star live-action depiction of Lewis Carroll's fantastic tale. The film featured an impressive, though somewhat confounding, array of actors: Charlotte Henry as Alice, W.C. Fields as Humpty Dumpty, Cary Grant as the Mock Turtle, Gary Cooper as the White Knight and Edna Mae Oliver as the Red Queen. The reissue of the Alice doll was a smart, practical move on Beatrice's part. It made good business sense to capitalize on the movie-going audience that might want a souvenir from their film experience. More scholarly texts than this one have analyzed how the movie business seemed to thrive in the

I n 1933, the bright lights of Tinseltown once again cast their lucky glow on a Madame Alexander creation. Beatrice wasn't alone in her devotion to the March sisters, the group that was seemingly becoming a talisman for the talented dollmaker. Stellar film director George Cukor selected the Louisa May Alcott classic as a vehicle for his favorite leading lady, Katharine Hepburn. The RKO motion picture benefited from an excellent, believable cast: Hepburn as Jo, Frances Dee as Meg, Jean Parker as Beth and Joan Bennett as Amy. Spring Byington was cast as the patient, stoic Marmee. Hepburn's depiction of ambitious, spirited Jo was a seamless blending of actress and role. This first big-screen telling of *Little Women* was an enormous box-office hit, and Madame Alexander's cloth line of March sisters was released in conjunction with the film. Granted a trademark of 344,080, the Alexander dolls were 16 inches in height, had pink muslin bodies and pressed-felt facial masks. They were very similar in design and costuming to the versions from the early 1930s for which Madame hadn't secured a copyright. The March sisters, their mother Marmee, and best friend/neighbor Laurie would all come to be made in various media throughout the next sixty-five years. Since 1933, a variation of the group has always been available from the Alexander Doll Company, with the exception of 1994, when a set of Little Women was held back in order to be released with a new 1995 film of the classic story.

Nineteen thirty-three was a prolific year for Beatrice and Philip, marked particularly by the mating of movies and dolls. Nowadays, film tie-ins are run-of-the-mill in the toy industry, but the Alexander achievements were ground-breaking in their day. Beatrice and Philip had been garbing already assembled composition doll bod-

Depression years, despite the daily collapsing of much more substantial, much more down-to-earth businesses. For a few pennies, care-worn people could forget their troubles and buy a ticket to paradise. The Hollywood "Dream Factories" thrived in these desperate times, and the Alexander Doll Company, though not as successful as the movie industry, managed to hold its own, too. Given her odds-defying survival, it is easy to understand why Madame Alexander observed decades later that: "Dolls are not a luxury. They are as necessary to a child's life as a loaf of bread." The 1930s had been marked by bread lines, cinema lines and doll lines.

ies, and at this point, they decided to mix and manufacture their own composition creations. The Alexander Doll Company's production of Walt Disney's The Three Little Pigs dolls began in earnest in 1933, and an association between Disney and the company continues to this day.

The movies were turning out to be a goldmine for the Alexander Doll Company, but there was one real-life character Beatrice rejected: Shirley Temple. Shirley was America's sweetheart. The perpetually cheerful child, with the golden ringlets and preternatural dimples, embodied an optimism that the Depression era lacked. She was a huge sensation in movie palaces from Connecticut to California. Mildred was now eighteen and married, and she was cognizant of the pint-size tap-dancing star's popularity. She recommended that a Shirley doll might be a beneficial addition to the Alexander line. "'Absolutely not,' my mother shot back," Mildred recalls. "She wasn't really aware of who Shirley was. She didn't think she was all that important." According to Mildred, Madame Alexander was convinced that Alice in Wonderland and Little Women had done well for the company because of their connection to the printed page. "She felt that they were classics. They were written for an intelligent readership. My mother honestly didn't know who Shirley Temple was. Remember, she was always working. She didn't have time to go to the picture shows. So, we never did an official Shirley Temple doll."

Morris Michtom and A. Cohn, the powers-that-be at rival Ideal Novelty and Toy Company, did not hesitate to jump on the Shirley bandwagon. Their composition model, sculpted by the talented, prolific Bernard Lipfert, was extremely popular. From 1934 to 1938, more than six million Shirley Temple dolls were bought in America. "In hindsight, we could kick ourselves," Mildred asserts. "My mother told me that she was very sorry that she hadn't listened to me." (In an interesting

side note, without invoking the dreaded name of Shirley Temple, the Alexander Doll Company did capitalize on the blonde moppet's success. In 1935 they issued a Little Colonel doll, ostensibly based on the book with that title written by Annie Fellows Johnston. The Alexander doll had dimples and Temple-like curls and it was released at the same time that the Shirley Temple movie of *The Little Colonel* was packing in the crowds. Also, in an interesting twist of fate, Madame ended up

Being scooped in the Shirley sweepstakes taught Madame Alexander a valuable lesson: popular culture *can* be the bedrock from which a classic doll grows.

hiring Bernard Lipfert in 1937 to sculpt a doll head based upon the face of Jane Withers, the number-six box-office star in the country, and the on-screen nemesis of Shirley Temple in countless films.)

Being scooped in the Shirley sweepstakes taught Madame Alexander a valuable lesson: popular culture *can* be the bedrock from which a classic doll grows. The Shirley Temple misstep remained a sore point throughout Madame's life. "When she would come to my house, I would have to hide my Shirley dolls," family friend Tanya McWhorter chuckles. "I would have to pick up all the Shirley dolls and throw them into the closet. She told me I should give them all away to charity. Oh, Madame hated Shirley Temple! Not the real, living Shirley, just her dolls," McWhorter adds.

It seems rather comical that into her nineties Madame Alexander would hold a grudge about "the one who got away," but her pride was bruised by that over-

In 1937 Gimbels Toy Department celebrated the second birthday of the Dionne Quintuplets with a display featuring the Alexander dolls in a variety of sizes.

⁂

sight. In many interviews granted during the 1960s and 1970s, Madame muses about the Temple trauma: "I was against the cashing-in on a child celebrity," she recalls, or she states, "I did not support the notion of exploiting a child." Alexander enthusiasts recognize back-pedaling when they hear it, for 1935 would usher in one of the greatest marketing coups ever centered around not just one child—but five!

On May 28, 1934, in the hamlet of Corbeil, a remote enclave of Ontario, Canada, the birth cries of five little sisters penetrated the gloom of an anxious world. Born two months prematurely, the Dionne quintuplets were hailed as a miracle and a sure sign that prosperity was just around the corner. Each infant girl—Yvonne, Annette, Cécile, Emilie and Marie—weighed less than two pounds, but their tiny stature merely added to the grand nature of their tale. They were the world's first-known surviving quints, and the newspapers and movie-reel news could not get enough of them. Their parents, Oliva and Elzire, were poor, simple people, and already the parents of five children: three boys and two girls. In the so-called best interest of the quintuplets, the Canadian government removed the newborn girls from their parents. Under the supervision of Dr. Allan Roy Dafoe, the Dionnes were made wards of the Ontario government, and were placed in a virtual theme park called Quintland, across the street from the family home in Corbeil.

In this fish-bowl environment, they were on display for as many as six thousand visitors a day, who came to watch them play and eat behind a one-way screen. Knowledge of, and contact with, the Dionnes was a coveted treasure. Dafoe worked out deals with advertisers and sponsors, selling the girls' likenesses to everything ranging from corn syrup to Quaker Oats. The fascination with the Dionne babies was an international obsession.

Madame Alexander and Philip recognized the five widely covered babes as perfectly suited for doll renderings. The peculiar aspects of the Dionnes' upbringing were decades from being questioned. In 1935, the infants were promoted and applauded as beacons of hope in a hopeless time. There was fierce competition for the rights to secure the official trademark of these novel children, but the Alexander Doll Company obtained from the Canadian trustees the coveted license to manufacture Dionne likenesses. (A line of

Superior Company Quints was sold very briefly in Canada circa 1935, but these authorized dolls did not achieve the same quality or popularity as the Alexander versions.) The first generation of Madame Alexander Dionne Quintuplet babies began to be advertised in the spring of 1935. The dolls were offered in various versions: 7 1/2-inch compositions with bent legs that allowed the dolls to sit but not stand, 17 1/2-inch cloth-bodied compositions, 23-inch cloth-bodied compositions, and an all-cloth depiction. A set of all five babies was offered with white enamel beds, kiddie cars and a carousel.

By March 1936, the Quints were featured in their "home." They came with nursery furniture and a doll embodying their attending nurse. (The name of the nurse who helped Dafoe deliver the Dionnes varies from publication to publication. In some books she is identified as Louise De Kirilene; in others she is called Yvonne Leroux.) Dr. Dafoe joined his female assistant as a doll in mid-1936, as well. (Strangely, many records and price listings of the Dafoe doll have his name incorrectly spelled as Defoe and DeFoe.) Both doctor and nurse were composition, and jointed at the hips and shoulders. They had mohair wigs, but their eyes were interpreted differently. Dafoe's eyes were painted; the nurse's were sleep eyes, which Madame claimed to be an Alexander innovation. Late that same year, the Quint-O-Bile was introduced, a contraption that allowed all five 7 1/2-inch dolls to swing, facing each other.

By 1937, the Dionnes were growing into toddlers, and the Alexander Doll Company kept pace. An 11 1/2-inch composition toddler was produced. It featured molded and painted hair, plus brown sleep eyes. Its upper lashes were human hair, but its brows and lower lashes were painted. It had straight legs that allowed it to stand unaided, and its feet were flat and had dimpled toes. Each of the five toddlers was identical in sculpting and in features; their only individuality was found in the color of their frock and bonnet. Cécile was exclusively garbed in green; Emilie in lavender; Annette in yellow; Marie in blue and Yvonne in pink. Toward the end of her life, Madame Alexander would recount to Tanya McWhorter what it was like to visit with the juvenile media darlings: "She hated the cold. She liked to be warm, and where the Dionnes lived, it was absolutely freezing. She and Philip had to wear red long johns the whole time they were up there." Madame Alexander also confided another quirky tidbit to Tanya: "She used to say that she was responsible for giving Yvonne her very first cold!"

Whether or not Madame was really responsible for infecting Yvonne with her first childhood ailment can-

The fascination with the Dionne Quintuplets became an international obsession; Madame recognized that the babies were perfectly suited for doll renderings.

not be proven, but the boast typifies Beatrice's need to elaborate, to brilliantly intertwine herself with the memorable dolls she was creating. Long before the Alexander Doll Company honored its founder with an official doll likeness on the occasion of her eighty-ninth birthday, and then again on her hundredth, Beatrice was carving out a line of dolls that embodied *her* passions, *her* preoccupations, *her* reading of the American public and even *her* own family. The beloved Wendy Ann face mold made its entrance in 1936, and the popular countenance, which continued to be produced until 1947, was named for Madame's infant granddaughter. Grandson William Birnbaum (whom Madame honored in 1957 by giving his name to the boy doll she had been

In 1939 FAO Schwarz introduced the Alexander Doll Company's Scarlett O'Hara with this lavish display of dolls, books and photos from the blockbuster movie.

producing since 1953) has observed with a mixture of exasperation and undeniable respect, "When you go through all the publicity that the company received over the years, most of the stories always focused on Madame. The reporters covered what she wore, how she stood, what she looked like. I would often say to her, 'How about getting some coverage on the dolls?' It was the dolls we were selling. We weren't selling her. But in the long run, she was correct. She was what made the dolls special; she was the story behind the dolls."

And what stories she had to tell! The 1937 securing of a trademark for Scarlett O'Hara and the other Pulitzer Prize-winning denizens of Margaret Mitchell's great American novel was the ultimate hybrid of creator and creation. When Beatrice purchased a copy of *Gone With the Wind* in 1936, the forty-one-year-old New Yorker was swept away. "My

mother read that book in a single weekend," Mildred reveals. "She sat down and stayed up throughout the night reading it. She asked Dorothy (her housekeeper) to make her a pot of tea and some toast, and she never put the book down. She barely stopped to eat."

Madame Alexander explained to reporters throughout her long career, "On Monday morning, after finishing the book, I went to work, and by Wednesday I had created a doll from the description of Scarlett in the novel. She had a heart-shaped face, a small nose, green eyes, black hair and was one of my prettiest doll characters." The visualization of Scarlett was an uncanny, almost prophetic portrait of actress Vivien Leigh. This

1936 prototype of Scarlett O'Hara was made two years before Leigh landed that plum role. The search for the perfect Scarlett made national headlines as starlets and established actresses endured screen tests and brutal costume fittings. Among the O'Hara "wannabes" who vowed "never to go hungry again" were Katharine Hepburn, Lana Turner, Tallulah Bankhead, Joan Crawford, Susan Hayward and Bette Davis! The list of aspiring Southern belles reads like an A-list of Hollywood royalty.

According to correspondence that Madame shared with some of her friends and business associates, she sent her conception of Scarlett to the executives at MGM who made no secret of their frustrated scouting for the perfect heroine. If Madame remembered accurately, three days after receiving her package, the MGM honchos sent back a contract for her to design and manufacture Scarlett dolls. She would remind her confidants that her Scarlett likeness was shipped off to MGM before Vivien Leigh was auditioned and cast. The resemblance between Leigh and the Alexander doll, as noted earlier, is remarkable, and Madame hinted that her interpretation colored the executives' final casting decision. The authenticity of the anecdote is debatable, however, because many Alexander historians have never been able to sort out whether she procured the rights for Scarlett from MGM or the author, Margaret Mitchell, directly.

Why did Scarlett O'Hara hold such an allure for Beatrice Alexander Behrman? "She saw herself in Scarlett," Mildred Behrman Birnbaum explains. "I personally couldn't see it, but she definitely did." The independent, never-say-die outlook of the Margaret Mitchell heroine does indeed parallel Madame Alexander's own optimistic, scrappy existence. And if Mildred's recollections from her sixteenth birthday can be believed, Madame Alexander even had the same innovative eye for window-treatments as Scarlett did. "Mother had an English seamstress named Sarah Ellis. She was making me a special dress, and it called for a lot of work on the hem. It needed a lot of attention, and the seamstress said she could use additional cord for the bottom of the dress. Yes, it needed lots of cord and trim." Mildred pauses mischievously in the telling of her tale. "Mother went to the window and pulled down the drapery. She took the cord right off the curtains. This was the

The Alexander Doll Company archives abound with still movie photos featuring the *Gone with the Wind* stars Clark Gable and Vivien Leigh, which were often used in store promotions such as the FAO Schwarz display on the opposite page.

dress for my sixteenth birthday!"

Mildred Behrman's Sweet Sixteen was in 1931—who's to say Margaret Mitchell had even begun penning that infamous drapery-dress scene? Without benefit of the book or movie, Madame had imitated Scarlett uncannily. The unsinkable ingenuity and stoic courage in the face of adversity demonstrated by both the Georgian vixen and the New York businesswoman certainly invite comparisons. Though Mildred didn't see a connection between the fictional character and her flesh-and-blood mother, she does admit, "Mother lived

In 1937, Madame Alexander fell under the spell of England's eleven-year-old princess, and created a Princess Elizabeth doll to commemorate her father's coronation.

her life in a brave way. When we moved from the Bronx to Gramercy Park in about 1928 or so, we had definitely taken a step up—not that we could actually afford it! But Mother had her pride."

By all accounts, she also had her looks. Dark-haired and brown-eyed, Madame was a petite woman, standing about 5 feet 2 inches tall, and never admitted to weighing more than 116 pounds. In this earlier era, when women were rarely prominent in the workplace, Beatrice stood out with her correct posture, beguiling smile and always dainty, feminine attire. Just as Scarlett had to battle a constant line of inappropriate suitors, Madame had her encounters with lecherous advances. "My grandmother was an attractive woman," William Birnbaum relays. "There's a story that I don't have all the details sorted out on. But it goes something like this....A female violin teacher and her son would come to the Gramercy Park apartment to give my mother,

Mildred, lessons. Well, the violin teacher's son was always giving Madame the eye. She didn't know how to handle the situation. She was becoming very uncomfortable and impatient. So, she decided that the best way to solve these unwelcome attentions was to break the violin! You see, this way she would eliminate the violin; she'd eliminate the teacher; and she'd eliminate the son. Problem solved! Maybe it wasn't the most rational way, but it was certainly effective."

This tempestuous, headstrong behavior smacks of Scarlett, but ironically, it wasn't the valiant, feisty side of the character that appealed to Madame. In conversations and interviews, she points to Scarlett's generosity as the trait that links them. When Scarlett is facing starvation and stumbles upon a carrot, she shares it with her faithful maid. It was that selfless act that most impressed Madame Alexander, who grew to be quite renowned for her own charitable donations, scholarship funds and philanthropic causes. (Family scrapbooks contain many letters of thanks from the Massachusetts Institute of Technology (M.I.T.), Brandeis University, the Jewish Theological Seminary and the Women's League of Israel, to name just a few beneficiaries of Madame's generosity.) The quintessential Southern Belle has remained a staple of the Alexander Doll Company throughout the ensuing decades. Even today, Scarlett's dark hair and flashing eyes grace the Alexander catalog.

Besides being touched by Scarlett fever, the year 1937 also witnessed the birth of the Princess Elizabeth face mold. Beatrice had fallen under the spell of England's Princess Elizabeth, the eleven-year-old monarch who was much photographed by newspapers and magazines. Elizabeth and her younger sister Margaret were the sub-

When Princess Elizabeth's father was crowned King George VI in 1937, the young monarch-to-be was also immortalized as an Alexander doll, and promoted as the future Queen of Dolls.

Make way for the
future Queen of Dolls-

PRINCESS ELIZABETH

As early as 1934 the Alexander
Doll Company was advertising their Tony Sarg marionettes. The
puppeteer himself promoted the toys by performing puppet shows at
stores like B. Altman & Co.

jects of royal watchers who were captivated by the real-life drama that was being played out in Britain. On January 20, 1936, Edward VIII reluctantly assumed the throne after the death of his father, King George V. Edward was not comfortable with the notion of being king; the weight of the crown was heavy upon his head. Not ideally suited for this position of enormous responsibility, and having become enamored of an American divorcee, Wallis Warfield Simpson, Edward abdicated on December 11, 1936, to marry the woman he loved.

This romantic, history-making move placed Edward's younger brother, George, in line for the throne. George and his wife, Elizabeth, were the parents of Elizabeth and Margaret Rose. The two young daughters were

DOLLS AND ANIMALS
designed by
BEATRICE ALEXANDER
together with
PAINTINGS OF DOLLS
March 18th - 30th, 1935
ARGENT GALLERIES
42 West 57th Street

almost magically transformed into princesses on that fateful December day, and the eldest, Elizabeth, suddenly became the next-in-line to rule the United Kingdom.

The young angelic girls surrounded by the pageantry of their father George VI's coronation were perfect vehicles for Beatrice's talents. On May 12, 1937, the press excitedly reported how Elizabeth was just like an American pre-teen. Beneath her regal royal gown the future queen wore a pair of popular, comfortable bobby socks! The Alexander Doll Company made a Princess Elizabeth doll to commemorate the king's coronation, and then used the lovely Princess Elizabeth countenance on the Snow White doll that was released in 1937 to coincide with the Walt Disney cartoon. The Princess Elizabeth face continued to be utilized on the company's creations throughout the decades as upper-class young ladies garbed in riding habits and party dresses, among other interpretations.

The wonderful world of Disney, with its wholesome family fare, was perfect for inspiring hands-on toys and at-home entertainment. Children who marveled at Mickey and Minnie's animated antics were understandably anxious to re-create the cartoon humor in their own living rooms. The Alexander Doll Company recruited Tony Sarg, a well-known illustrator and master puppeteer. Born in Guatemala, the son of a German consul, Sarg had studied marionette carving and operating with the Holden Troupe, and then branched out to form his own studio and performing group. In late 1937 he began to create Walt Disney marionette and play theaters that were exclusively manufactured by the Alexander Doll Company. These marionettes were, as

the 1941 catalog copy reads, "ingenuously adopted [sic] so that a youngster can manipulate and animate these marionettes with one hand." (As an interesting side note, Sarg was also responsible for masterminding the gas-filled balloons that comprise the Macy's Thanks-giving parade in New York City. His creative, inventive life was cut short in 1942.)

The 1930s deserve such in-depth analysis because this decade epitomized the heart and soul of the early Alexander Doll Company. The company was tested by the Depression and the specter of possible financial ruin. Due to its founder's resolve and resourcefulness, however, it survived brilliantly. So brilliantly, in fact, that in a 1936 article on American doll companies, the business magazine *Fortune* featured Madame Alexander along with Effanbee and Ideal, pinpointing the three as the major American dollmakers of the era. The appearance of this article is an important documentation of the stature Madame Alexander had achieved with her young doll company.

This same ten-year period opened up Beatrice's eyes to the power of headlines and deadlines. She learned to curry the favor of newspaper columnists and reporters, discovering that a well-placed story and quote can boost a tenuous position. For a time, she even wrote a syndicated newspaper column, in which she shared her hints for entertaining and her recipes. The columns bore titles like "Plans for an Alice in Wonderland Party" and "An English Actress Plans Our Menu." On the business side, she went out of her way to meet the shipping requirements and inventory requests of major department-store clients. Most effectively, with Scarlett and Princess Elizabeth, she learned the power of the movie palace and the appeal of Buckingham Palace, two lessons she would not forget.

Triumph and Acclaim

The 1940s were a hectic, challenging time for Madame Alexander. Beatrice found herself repeating her best moves of the 1930s and dismissing her faltering steps. She continued to pay homage to famous movie personalities and well-known public figures: Olympic figure skater Sonja Henie, child star Margaret O'Brien, Academy Award winner Ginger Rogers and Broadway sensation Mary Martin were just some of the popular performers created in doll form during the 1940s. Innovation was the name of the game in the 1940s; Beatrice introduced the Jeannie Walker doll in 1942. As the name suggests, Jeannie was one of the toy industry's first walking dolls.

The triumphs and big sellers that the Alexander Doll Company was achieving during the 1940s translated exponentially into the need for more square feet. As the line expanded and

the demand for additional inventory accelerated, Beatrice and Philip looked for additional warehouse and factory space. The company that originated in a kitchen, and then expanded to a storefront, sought out additional showrooms, office suites and factory buildings. In a September 1957 interview, Madame touted her more than fifteen hundred employees and her three factories, two situated in New York City and one in White Plains, New York. Eventually the three factories were consolidated into a single building in the Harlem section of Manhattan, where the company remains headquartered today. Nowadays, in addition to the Harlem-based factory and corporate offices, there is a showroom located in Manhattan's Toy Center on Fifth Avenue, where retailers go to see the year's offerings, and where special events and press conferences are held.

The Depression had threatened Beatrice's dreams in the decade past, and now the 1940s were ablaze with World War II. Rationing and a reduction in available materials were hurdles that Madame had to clear, and she did so with style. Perhaps she didn't have

In 1941 the Alexander Doll Company issued a four-page black-and-white catalog featuring Wendy-Ann on the cover. Inside, Madame's dolls were inspired by children's books, Disney movies and even Buckingham Palace.

Above: In the late 1940s Madame presented entertainer Mary Martin with a doll depicting her in a sailor suit. Left: The company's 1942-43 catalog had grown to eight pages; it introduced Jeannie Walker and included the Kate Greenaway dolls and a two-doll set called Mother and Me.

the quantity of fabrics or trimmings that she would have preferred, but Beatrice was "brought up to do more than just make do." As she told the *National Jewish Monthly* in a February 1966 interview, "It's customary to think of lace and embroidery as synonymous with wealth. But even the poorest of immigrant women needed and created beauty. They made and embroidered

their own underwear, crocheted edgings on their petticoats. As I think back to my childhood, there were few Jewish households that didn't have at least a few sheets and pillowcases trimmed with hand-made lace." Despite restrictions and limitations, she would not allow the dolls that bore her name to emerge from her factory looking anything less than well dressed and well tended.

In honor of the United States' Armed Forces, the

Madame enjoyed a rare quiet moment in her elegant home in the 1940s.

Madame enjoyed a rare quiet moment in her elegant home in the 1940s.

Alexander Doll Company created a patriotic line of military personnel: soldiers, WAACs, WAVEs and an Armed Forces doll. These composition creations with their tailored, non-frilly uniforms are a jarring departure from the beribboned, flower-festooned sweethearts that continued, even at that time, to spell out Alexander. With news that the Allied troops were heading toward an inevitable, long-awaited German surrender, Beatrice put out a Miss Victory doll in 1944. This composition doll had blue sleep eyes and an open mouth. She wore star-spangled colors: a white blouse decorated with blue trim, and a red skirt. In her hands, the FAO Schwarz Company placed a magnet, which enabled her to hold a flag to celebrate the country's triumph.

The post-World War II years were prosperous ones for the nation as a whole, and for Madame Alexander in particular. Often called the "Golden Age of Dolls," those years "were wonderful, affluent ones," dealer Lia Sargent comments. "Everything that was made during those incredible years couldn't be made that way again. Today, the labor costs are too high, and the materials just aren't used." (Today, dolls from this era are often worth thousands of dollars.)

Madame Alexander would most likely second Sargent's enthusiasm. From 1946 to 1955, the Alexander Doll Company became a wellspring of high ideals and high fashion. Beatrice's childhood aspirations and inspirations were fully realized in this exceptional era. There must have been many mornings when the dollmaker awoke and pinched herself long and hard—she had managed to make her childhood dreams come true.

Many magnificent and prized creations were produced during this era, beginning with the 1946 debut of the 21-inch Portrait Series of dolls. Extremely ornate in their costuming and painting, the Portrait dolls were renderings of film heroines, opera and ballet principals, artists' muses, public figures, literary characters and members of royalty. They sold for an astonishing seventy-five dollars. (In 1946 a respectable weekly salary was sixty dollars.) The first twelve Portrait dolls were: the June Bride; Carmen; Mary Louise; Renoir; the Groom; Judy; King; Queen; Camille; Orchard Princess; Princess Rosetta and Rebecca. These dolls utilized either the Wendy Ann mold, which had debuted in 1936, or the Margaret mold, which was created in 1946, used on many different designs, and widely regarded as the company's most beautiful face. Also, in this very productive year, Karen Ballerina—the cover girl for this book—debuted. The composition version of Karen Ballerina was available in three sizes: 15, 18 and 21 inches. She sported what collectors today refer to as the Margaret facial sculpt which, at the time of its introduction, was based upon the popular child actress of the day, Margaret O'Brien. (Karen Ballerina was redone in a hard-plastic version in 1948 and 1949.)

If box-office receipts measure success, Margaret O'Brien was never as big a star as Shirley Temple. O'Brien wasn't a cheerful, hands-on-her-hips, wind-up toy of a girl. Rather, she was dark-haired, often wan of complexion and extremely intense. If Shirley was loved for her jubilant, upbeat personality, Margaret became a

household sensation because of her ability to tug on the heartstrings. At the age of seven, she received a Special Oscar as Outstanding Child Actress for her part in *Meet Me in St. Louis*, the musical valentine to the talents of Judy Garland, directed by Garland's husband, Vincente Minelli.

Perhaps Madame seized upon Margaret because she was such an antithesis to Shirley, or maybe it just made solid dollar-and-cents sense. Prior to 1946, Margaret appeared in nine films, among the most successful were *Journey for Margaret*, *Jane Eyre* and *The Canterville Ghost*. Her Alexander likeness came in three eye-color choices: hazel, brown and blue, and three hair shades: dark brown, reddish brown and, in 1947, dark ash blond.

Madame once again attempted to launch herself into the world of children's fashions via the Margaret doll. She created a line of juvenile clothing to complement the doll's outfits;

Child star Margaret O'Brien was the model for the hard-plastic doll that bore her name, which was advertised in this 1948 store catalog.

this attempt to branch out into children's clothing lasted one year, from 1946 to 1947.

Composition, which had proven itself to be a successful medium for the Alexander Doll Company, was now retired after two decades of performance. Beatrice and Philip turned to the wonders of a new "miracle" product: plastic. From 1947 through 1949, Philip worked alongside chemical engineers to help devise a formula that would translate well into doll production. Plastic was preferable to composition because moisture and temperature changes would not crack the dolls' surfaces. Its disadvantage was that it was not as porous as composition and, therefore, did not retain the high-color finishes of facial and torso painting. In the *Antiques Journal* of May 1972, Madame recalled her and her husband's early forays into plastic as "unpredictable, and [product] was apt to come out spotted. On a doll, that was disastrous." With a touch of modesty and good

In 1949 Madame created a set of Little Women *based upon the actresses who starred in the film of that year. This company photo shows a later version of the set, which can be dated to 1951 because the dolls wear Fashion Academy wrist tags, rather than the original clover-leaf tags, and because of the change in Amy's hairstyle.*

humor, she confided to her interviewer that the successful outcome was entirely accidental. In 1947, considered by Alexander experts to be a "transitional year" between composition and hard plastic, the first face mold to utilize the new medium was the Margaret O'Brien doll.

Madame's belief in, and pioneering use of, plastic set the tone for the rest of the toy industry. There was an advertising slogan of the day that promised "better living through chemistry," and the Alexander company demonstrated great faith in the untried, wide-open avenues of science. Utilizing the new technology from DuPont, Madame had chosen hard plastic to be the medium for her dolls. According to Lia Sargent, Madame "demonstrated the American spirit to embrace new ideas and new techniques. Unlike bisque and composition, hard plastic was durable, and highly defined features were molded with precision dies." When the competitors saw the fabulous results that the Alexander Doll Company was able to reach via plastics, this experimental material became the industry-wide choice.

The achievements of the Alexander Doll Company during the late 1940s were especially remarkable because the company was utilizing the services of a common factory, Model Plastics in White Plains, New York, along with the Arranbee Doll Company and the American Character Doll Company. Model

In 1950 Cinderella was advertised and promoted heavily by stores like John Wanamaker's in Philadelphia, where inventive displays for the doll and her Prince Charming were created.

Plastics was a joint venture under triple ownership of the three companies, and produced plastic body and limb molds, and rather similar face molds, for all three enterprises. The panache of the Alexander dolls was accomplished through their unique costume designs and their detailed painting and accessorizing. Alexander doll authority and well-regarded author A. Glenn Mandeville states, "The wigging and the clothing are what established the Alexander dolls' characters. From one single plastic face mold, like Wendy, for instance, she was able to spawn a million different looks. As a collector, you see past the similarity of the faces and you suspend your disbelief. You accept that Wendy is a farmer, then a soldier, then Scarlett, then a first-grader. You buy into the wardrobe and the identity of

In March 1951, Emil Hartman, director of the New York Fashion Academy awarded the Fashion Academy's gold medal to Madame Alexander for the first time.

each and every doll." In its seventy-five-year history the Alexander Doll Company has manufactured more than six thousand different dolls from a figurative handful of face molds.

As the 1950s dawned, Madame Alexander was likewise in her fifth decade. She had spent nearly thirty years as the driving force behind a thriving, booming business. And "booming" was quite the operative word. The soldiers who returned home from the European and Pacific Theaters married and settled down. The children who were born to these former fighting men comprised the Baby Boomer generation. It doesn't require a Census Bureau actuary to add up the numbers: a flood of newborn babes meant a wave of doll-less little girls had just entered the world. Madame Alexander and her thriving company were there to fill that need. The Fifties have been chronicled as Fabulous Happy Days. The United States was

flexing its muscles as the first bona-fide Super Power, and the nation's future seemed limitless.

The national landscape never seemed so serene, and confidence in our country's leaders and policies was always reported in the newspapers as 100 percent A-Okay. Families aspired for better lives, and under the G.I. bill, returning servicemen were granted federally funded mortgages, educational grants and business loans. Tract houses and suburban subdivisions were built to ensure that these working men who worked so hard to attain white-collar respectability would have private backyards, one-car garages and white picket fences to come home to. Being middle class had never felt so good, nor had there ever been such bounty to choose from. The Alexander Doll Company honed in on this notion of a businessman's home being his castle, and his primly dressed daughters, his little princesses. "During the 1950s, you find that a lot of the Alexander catalogs are written in this very Anglo style," Lia Sargent explains. "There are characters serving tea to Mummy and attending the Devon horse show, in a very English style, along the lines of what Ralph Lauren does today with his ads." Designed to appeal to up-and-coming executives and their home-maker wives, the Alexander promotional material worked brilliantly. The Alexander dolls were presented as the best, "the Cadillacs of dolldom," to borrow a phrase from the *Christian Science Monitor*. The dolls were garbed in costuming of impeccable quality, and the "Madame" on their packaging lent a fashionable European seal of approval to these superior American-made dolls.

The 1950s were a productive time for the Alexander family business. Beatrice, Philip and their son-in-law, Richard Birnbaum, were ensconced in an industry that is often perceived as faddish and novelty-ish. They continued to steer their corporation away from inferior merchandise. One of the first lines of dolls that debuted in 1950 was the 14-inch Godey series. These hard-plastic interpretations of the illustrations that graced *Godey's Lady's Book*, a Philadelphia-based women's periodical that began in 1830, had been received well in their circa-1945 composition incarnations, and now Madame hoped that the new plastic medium and the abundance of higher quality fabrics would make these Victorian-themed dolls extremely sought after.

Her attention to even the smallest detail, designing costumes that not only draped a doll but elevated it, caught the attention of the Fashion Academy. In 1951, this prestigious body of professionals and pundits bestowed their Gold Medal upon her. It was the first of four consecutive acknowledgments; in 1952, 1953 and 1954, she would receive this top honor again and again

Madame posed with some of her 1951 dolls and her Fashion Academy Gold medal. She was to win this top honor three more times.

and again. The 1951 ceremony at which Madame was presented with her award took place at the Alexander Doll Company's Fifth Avenue showroom, and was attended by toy buyers, press representatives, family and friends. The speech that preceded the award presentation is a glorious summation of Beatrice Alexander Behrman's life and times: "By dressing Alexander dolls in clothes that are lovely in fabric and exquisite in design, you have not alone made them enchanting and precious in themselves, but you have helped to stimulate in our younger generation an exciting interest in fashion and a growing awareness of style. For reflecting the ultimate in design beauty, for encouraging good taste and clothes appreciation, and for symbolizing 'best dressed' so perfectly, Alexander dolls are truly deserving of this tribute."

A. Glenn Mandeville believes that the recognition from the Fashion Academy was an especially satisfying accolade for Madame. "A lot of collectors call Madame Alexander a doll artist—that's not what she was. She was a clothing designer who draped her dreams on her dolls. When she won those medals, she was competing against designers who were creating clothing for actual living, breathing people. Imagine how staggering and almost unbelievable those victories must have been."

The charmed 1950s were full of additional crowning achievements. The royal family of Britain was once again in the American newspapers in 1953. Little Princess Elizabeth was now a married woman of twenty-seven, preparing to ascend to the throne of England. The fanfare and pageantry that surrounded this age-old custom was enthralling for monarch-less Americans. The country had seemingly gone crown-crazy. Merchandise was manufactured relentlessly to capitalize on the coronation theme: Elizabeth Arden Cosmetics produced a Coronation Pink lipstick; Nestlé sponsored contests and sweepstakes in which the winners would be flown to London for the coronation; Pepperell Manufacturing Company marketed bed sheets tied in to the royal theme, and the Alexander Doll Company released a series of 18-inch hard-plastic Beaux Arts dolls, tributes to the royal family and other nobles of the time. Pandemonium and media hyperbole surrounded the impending event. The British Trade Promotion Center attempted to work out deals with department stores across all forty-eight states, and only Arizona declined to participate. Retail giants like Wanamaker, Gimbels and Macy's had in-store promotions and public-relations giveaways.

The Brooklyn-based department store Abraham & Straus (A & S) was a grande dame of retail venues. Built like a cathedral with high domed ceilings, thick carpeted floors leading to shiny marble corridors, and sparkling chandeliers hanging above the well-heeled patrons, it was an elegant, affluent store located in the heart of downtown Brooklyn. Though A & S was a mecca for well-to-do New Yorkers, featuring a tea room where "ladies who lunch" gath-

In honor of Queen Elizabeth's coronation, Madame Alexander created a 36-doll dramatization of The Coronation Story, which was exhibited at Brooklyn's A & S department store.

Scenes from Madame's Coronation tableau included: top: The playing of *God Save the Queen* as the Archbishop of Canterbury approaches, holding the great crown of St. Edward; above: The Westminster Choir Boys; left: The Archbishop preparing to bestow the crown.

Madame oversaw each step of the creation of the Coronation dolls, down to examining each accessory. Below: In the Recessional, Her Majesty is attended by daughters of Peers appointed by her for this honor.

ered, the notion of a Brooklyn store hopping aboard the bandwagon to honor a British queen struck the media as headline-worthy. Skeptical eyes turned toward this promised extravaganza, and when the exhibit opened, they were amazed by the authentic, regal tribute that occurred.

In November 1952, seven months before the ceremony's June 2, 1953, date, A & S public relations executive, Frances Bemis (sometimes identified as Francis Bingham), who maintained a lifelong friendship with Madame, had approached the dollmaker with the request to create the complete pomp and circumstance

Madame Alexander's 36-doll rendering of the Coronation story drew more than 7,000 visitors on the exhibition's opening day at A & S.

in doll form. Always fascinated with palace pageantry, Madame immediately agreed to accept the commission and threw herself into the research of what occurs at a Westminster Abbey affair. This undertaking took so much out of Madame that she reported to friends and family that she would periodically burst into tears. She was placing a great amount of pressure on herself to do justice to this very special ceremony. Even though certain articles of clothing would never be seen by the public because they would be hidden by layers of overgarments, Madame could not let cheap, incorrect substitutes go by. Philip, concerned for his wife's welfare, suggested that she abandon these compulsive high standards but Madame refused. Eventually, it is said, she had a wall erected to protect her work station from prying eyes and contradictory tongues.

The finished set of thirty-six dolls depicts Queen Elizabeth II leaving the palace for the coronation, as well as her exit from the Abbey with six maids of honor carrying the train of her robe. It also captures the archbishops, choir boys, royal relatives and honor guards who attended the various functions. The dolls are set against six tableaux that were built, painted and wallpapered to exactly match the true locations. Fifty-five members of the A & S department store's window-dressing team worked around the clock to construct the authentic sets, and Madame matched them seam by seam, bead by bead, in her detailing. She drew once again upon her academic background and worked closely with Doris Langley Moore of the British Museum of Costume. They were able to second-guess much of the wardrobe and accompanying sundries based upon the rules of proper dress dictated by Bluemantle Pursuivant of Arms, a member of College of Arms that was founded in the 1200s. They were also able to obtain the cloth for the robes from the same mill that had turned out the actual coronation mantles.

The completed garbing of the thirty-six figures was so convincing that CBS television used the Alexander figures to act out the much anticipated ceremony on the air. This was before the days of satellite link-ups, and the religious aspects of the ceremony prevented camera crews from recording the event in its entirety. Instead, CBS hired a narrator who led the television viewers through the coronation one day before competing television stations received the abridged film. The publicity generated by the Alexander dolls' TV performance turned the A & S exhibit into a must-see show that rivaled Rodgers and Hammerstein's *The King and I*, playing to SRO audiences on the other side of the Manhattan Bridge. Seven thousand people jammed into the exhibit area on the first day, and the miniature monarchs were held over on display for a week. At the end of their run, the one-of-a-kind set was donated to the Brooklyn Children's Museum. Valued then at an astounding $25,000, the dolls were initially offered to the Metropolitan Museum of Art for their permanent collection, but the arrangements could not be worked out. The Brooklyn Children's Museum, the world's oldest museum dedicated to the education and celebration of children, was founded in 1899, just four years after Beatrice was born in that New York City borough. It's quite fitting that these historic elaborate effigies have found a home in Madame's birthplace. (And those Alexander aficionados who have a keen eye for facial sculpting have noted that Cissy, who was not slated to make her public entrance until 1955, makes a cameo appearance as at least one of the Queen's attendees!)

The Coronation dolls were a high point of 1953, which in hindsight was quite a banner year for Madame. During this single year, the 18-inch Glamour Girls series debuted; a line of Peter Pan dolls was launched to commemorate the film's release; and the Alexanderkins were brought into the marketplace. The Alexanderkins were 7 1/2-inch and 8-inch dolls, primarily costumed in little-girl outfits, with a few dressed as brides, Southern belles, etc. These popular dolls debuted as straight-legged nonwalkers, and for the next two decades were manufactured as straight-legged walkers, bent-knee walkers and bent-knee nonwalkers. Since 1973 they have continued to be manufactured as straight-legged nonwalkers. In 1954-55 a few Alexanderkins were introduced as Storybook characters, but probably the best known of these diminutive creations are the Storybook, Americana and International collections introduced in the 1960s. Production of these small hard-plastic dolls in these themes continues today.

The world's first full-figured, high-heel-wearing fashion doll made her official debut in 1955, two years after the Coronation vignette (and four years before Barbie!). Though she played a small role in the royal pageantry (some witnesses say she was a maid of honor and a dancer; others say she was represented as just a maid of honor), no one can deny the impact she had when she met the world as plain and not-at-all-simple Cissy. Standing 20 (later 21) inches tall, she featured a fully jointed body, and arched feet to accommodate her high heels. Her eyebrows were feathered and her complexion was wholesome and flawless. (The head had been used on the more childishly developed Binnie

Walker.) Cissy was a well-coiffed, exquisitely brought-up young lady. She was a debutante, the breed of young lady who was equally at home sitting beside Mum at a society tea or chatting with an old friend of the family's at the races. Madame Alexander described the public's infatuation with Cissy as follows: "Every little girl dreams of being grown-up. There isn't anyone who hasn't seen a child walking around in mother's high heels. A bra, too, and a dress or negligee can turn a humdrum play day into a wonderful land of make-believe for a child. Cissy is the newest and most exciting doll in the world."

The guiding principles behind Cissy were childhood reveries and revelations. Little girls will one day blossom into mature women, and the Cissy doll aimed to set a good example of etiquette and appropriate attire. In dozens of candid interviews throughout her career, Madame had been known to say that "a child should see at an early age how important it is to wear well-fitting clothes in becoming colors. Even in the underpinnings of my costumes, I never use a safety pin. Adult garments would have a snap, wouldn't they? The first thing a little girl does is undress a doll. It just wouldn't do for her to receive the impression that the hem of a slip can be fixed with a safety pin, or that a lady doesn't wear stockings at all times. That wouldn't give her a basis for good grooming."

A comical anecdote that Miss Frances and Kathleen Blotney Birnbaum delight in sharing proves just how devoted Madame was to the concept of flawless grooming. According to their accounts, Madame once got up from her desk to greet a pair of buttoned-down bankers. As she crossed the floor to shake their hands, resplendent in pastel blouse, sherbet-colored skirt and complementary sweater, the waistband of her underpants came undone. Madame's pastel panties slid down her hips and dropped to her ankles. Without missing a beat, she looked both men in the eyes and said, "You see, gentlemen, it's true. I really do match from my head down to my toes!"

On the subject of undergarments, Sylvia Varon, a personal friend of Madame's, also has an eyebrow-raising revelation. "Madame was getting frustrated when a pair

Yardley products for America are created in England and finished in the U.S.A. from the original English formulae, combining imported and domestic ingredients. Yardley of London, Inc., 6

Makes you feel so fresh and feminine

Yardley English Lavender is more than a lovely, lingering fragrance.
It's a quick-change to a happy mood . . . makes you feel fresh,
gay, wonderful—like being in love. Enjoy it in many forms.
You'll find Yardley English Lavender at any cosmetic counter.
Essence, from $1.25 plus tax. Soap, box of three, $1.50.

Yardley Lavender

MADAME ALEXANDER

Opposite page: In July 1956 Cissy starred in this Yardley ad. Above: As elegant as Cissy herself, Madame appeared at a Hudson's store promotion in Michigan in 1957.

of stockings kept falling down on one of her dolls. As much as she tried to keep them up, they would slide down. So, she came up with the idea of sewing the silk stockings to the doll's panties. And by doing that, she invented panty hose! She never got credited with that invention, but Madame told me how she was the first to come up with that solution. The world has denied Madame her proper credit for that innovation."

In 1956 and 1957, the Cissy doll was used in ads for Yardley toiletries and cosmetics that appeared in magazines like *Ladies' Home Journal* and *McCall's*. Though she had a sophisticated trousseau and a mature fashion sense, Cissy was designed to be a good role model, keep-

ing with Madame's philosophy of dollmaking: Dolls should look like children and children should look like dolls. Despite her adult physique, the 1955 Cissy, who remained in the line until 1962, reflects the audience that the Alexander dolls of that time were being created for: children who handled, inspected, played with and loved their dolls. The adult collectors who today look for these vintage designs on the secondary market are not the audience that Madame imagined when she first began her self-appointed mission. "Dolls should contribute to a child's understanding of people, other times and other places," she often proclaimed. "Dolls should develop an appreciation of art and literature in a child. A doll can undoubtedly become a child's best friend," she would conclude.

The original Cissy and her scaled-down 9-inch companion Cissette, which debuted in 1957, certainly don't represent Madame Alexander's swan song, for the tireless professional still had thirty more years of creativity stretching before her. Madame was already sixty-two years old, three years away from retirement for the average American, but Madame had proved that she was not average. She continued to stay involved in her company's activities for the next three decades.

In the 1960s it may have seemed to some Americans that Cissy had found her way to the most famous house in the land. Jack and Jackie Kennedy were in the White House, and Camelot was no longer a myth. A ruggedly handsome president and his svelte, classy bride were the figures that Americans emulated and admired, and indeed, Jacqueline Bouvier Kennedy was almost like a Cissy doll in the flesh. Always adorned with tasteful jewelry that never clashed with her stylish suits or breathtaking gowns, Jackie was a rich debutante who did more than just stand graciously beside her husband on black-tie receiving lines. She could speak several languages, had been a photographer for a Washington daily newspaper and was a champion horsewoman. No wonder that Madame felt compelled to turn her and daughter Caroline into dolls. The 21-inch Jacqueline and 15-inch Caroline were made only in 1961 and 1962. Madame had often said that she stopped production on those two very successful creations because the Kennedys' press secretary, Pierre Salinger, personally asked her to cease production. Though she was the First Lady of dolls, Madame recognized that a presidential veto had to be obeyed.

Madame Alexander produced 21-inch Jackie and 15-inch Caroline in 1961 and 1962 only. She explained that Kennedy press secretary Pierre Salinger asked her to cease production.

Madame also realized in early 1961 that a lot of her customers didn't really believe she existed. They thought she was a corporate logo, a Betty Crocker of toyland. "I plead guilty to that, as well," states granddaughter-in-law Kathleen Blotney Birnbaum. "When I was a little girl, I received Madame Alexander dolls for birthdays and for Christmas. I remember asking my mother, did such a person really exist? We thought she was a made-up name. Imagine how I felt when I actually met her face-to-face one day." To combat that mythical status, the Alexander Doll Company launched a campaign on the back of their 1961 catalog that emphatically stated: "In answer to all the inquiries that we receive day after day, we would like to tell you, 'Yes, there is really truly a Madame Alexander, and she does indeed design and supervise the manufacture of her lovely dolls and their exquisitely made apparel.'"

"Exquisitely made apparel" became a touchstone for Beatrice during the 1960s. Once again she resurrected her never-ending fascination with dressing little girls, as well as their playthings. In 1960 she launched Madame Alexander Togs, a childrenswear apparel line that was sold in FAO Schwarz, Lord & Taylor and other upscale department stores. In several newspaper articles from the early 1960s, Madame explains that "friends have been urging me to make children's clothes for years. Even total strangers would write to me, asking, 'Why can't children look like your dolls?'"

THE WHITE HOUSE
WASHINGTON

June 12, 1967

Dear Madame Alexander:

What a dear and thoughtful person you are! The christening doll, with its own satin pillow, is the loveliest I have ever seen and will surely become a family heirloom. And I am just charmed with those two darling "muffins."

It is thrilling just to look at these exquisite creations of your artistry and anticipate the happiness they will bring to our first grandchild. I know Luci will be just as excited with this lovely gift as I am and joins me in warm thanks.

I, too, enjoyed meeting you at the luncheon. What a joy it must be to know that your wonderful talent has brought so much happiness to others.

With appreciation and every good wish,

Sincerely,

Lady Bird Johnson
Mrs. Lyndon B. Johnson

Madame Alexander
315 Oxford Road
New Rochelle, New York 10804

On May 5, 1967, the first lady of dolls met the First Lady of the United States, Lady Bird Johnson. Mrs. Johnson wrote Madame a month later to thank her for a gift for daughter Luci, who was expecting her first child.

In a 1963 *New York Times* profile of the doll manufacturer turned clothing designer, the juvenile clothing is extolled as "daintily decked with rickrack, appliquéd with tiny sailboats or parasols. Each outfit is packed with at least two toys. Some of the sets are made with reversible tops lined in clear plastic so that baby can eat and still look neat." Madame chimes in that she "tried to make the outfits both pretty and practical. I'm only doing what all little girls do," Madame explained to the reporter, "going from dolls and doll clothes to making things for real-live babies."

This final foray into children's fashions lasted for six

years; in 1966 Madame closed the doors on Madame Alexander Togs and concentrated exclusively on doll apparel. Grandson William Birnbaum explains, "She was given a choice. I won't say an ultimatum, but she was presented with a choice by my grandfather and her other business associates. She couldn't spread herself thin; she had to decide on the dolls or on the children's clothing. They felt she wasn't able to juggle both business ventures, and one or the other would suffer. She selected the dolls because that was the business she knew best." Birnbaum wistfully adds, "It was a shame that had to happen. She needed to control the designs of the clothing company, and she wouldn't consider licensing out her name. I think we could have achieved great things in the fashion world if we had been

around longer."

Choosing dolls meant that Madame had to maintain her indefatigable quest of always keeping her finger on the pulse of the populace. She mined the funny papers and television sitcoms for potential gold. Brenda Starr, ace reporter and comic-strip heroine, was given the Alexander treatment in 1964, and Gidget, immortalized on TV by Sally Field, saw the light of day in 1966. Both Brenda Starr and Gidget lasted a mere one year in the Alexander line. Still hoping to have a contemporary, with-it hit, Madame made a *That Girl* doll in 1967. The Marlo Thomas comedy is an especially revealing selection because it's a microcosm of the Alexander Doll Company's place in the so-called Swinging Sixties. The Marlo Thomas character, Ann Marie, was the first woman on television who was allowed to be single and to live on her own. An aspiring actress, who resided in a Manhattan apartment, Ann Marie was seemingly self-sufficient. Yet, when a temporary job turned sour or a theatrical producer's comments became too crushing, she always turned to her father, Lou Marie, a successful restaurateur in Brewster, New York, or Donald Hollinger, her stalwart, supportive boyfriend. Despite efforts at being independent, she was a girl-child, a bit dated and absurd, out of synch with a country that was being torn apart and tormented by the Vietnam War.

Student protests, a rise in drug use, draft dodging and draft-card burning—times were volatile. And it was difficult for Madame and her company to keep up with the new politics and the new revolutions. Philip, her husband and

Madame was photographed with her daughter, Mildred, who became a well-regarded painter, at an art gallery in Florida in the 1970s.

help mate for fifty-four years, died in 1966, and Madame now worked beside her son-in-law, Richard, and her grandson, William. With Philip Behrman's death, Richard took on responsibility for the day-to-day decisions of the Alexander Doll Company. He worked closely with William through the 1970s until his retirement in the early 1980s, when he handed all the responsibilities over to his son.

Madame had endured the death of many loved ones: her father; mother; sisters; an eleven-month-old child from a sweeping epidemic; and her precious granddaughter, Wendy Ann, in the mid 1950s, when she was barely twenty years old. (As a matter of fact, it was Wendy Ann's untimely death that prompted the Alexander Doll Company in 1955 to discard the "Ann" from the Wendy Ann doll's name. From that date on, the doll was simply known as Wendy, an abbreviation that softened Madame's pain.) The loss of her hus-

After the death of her husband, Madame relied on her son-in-law, Richard Birnbaum (on her left in photo), and her grandson, William Birnbaum, to direct the company with her.

band hit her hard, and she tried to distract herself with work, supervising her employees, who now numbered eleven hundred, but she wasn't always certain what the public wanted or needed. Forsaking the usual rosy-cheeked youngster of her doll line, she introduced something different: the Grandma Jane doll. Advertised as a modern grandma, she was dressed in a blue linen costume, featuring a silver coiffure and rimmed eyeglasses. Madame hoped that this senior-citizen rendering would help teach respect toward elders, and patch up the friction that was tearing the country apart. The Grandma Jane doll was laden with good intentions, which, however, did not translate into tangible sales.

During Christmas week in 1969, a quote from Madame Alexander popped up in newspapers through-

out the country. "My dolls don't roller skate; they don't do backbends; they don't blow plastic bubbles. A doll should stimulate a child's imagination and move the child to action. Do we want the doll to perform and the child to sit there? Isn't it healthier to have the child perform and the doll sit still?" Madame Alexander posed this question, and the wire services ran with it. Sharing newspaper space with this doll declaration were reports of the first draft lottery since World War II being held in New York City, Op-Ed responses to Lieutenant William

Calley being charged with pre-meditated murder in the My Lai massacre and President Nixon ordering all stockpiles of germ warfare to be destroyed. It was quite a different world from the one in which Madame had designed patriotic soldier dolls. America was restless as assassinations and civil unrest became daily footnotes to the evening news.

For the Alexander Doll Company, the 1960s are remembered for the tributes that Beatrice began to receive on an almost daily basis. Margaret Winson established the Madame Alexander Fan Club in 1961; its name later changed to the Madame Alexander Doll Club and it was incorporated as a not-for-profit corporation in Illinois. (Today, with its membership numbering twelve thousand, it no longer holds not-for-profit status.) She was honored on United Nations Day in 1965. At New York's City Hall, US Ambassador Arthur Goldberg presided over the unveiling of her complete line of International dolls. The Smithsonian Institution placed two Madame Alexander dolls into their permanent collection: the Madame Doll from the American Revolution series, based on the Frances Cavanah book, *The Secret of the Madame Doll*, and the Scarlett O'Hara doll.

The placement of Beatrice Alexander Behrman's work into the Smithsonian Institution was a grand achievement for the little girl who was raised on Grand Street above a doll hospital. Having weathered the societal upheavals of the 1960s, and the competition from more aggressive doll companies of that era and their Saturday-morning-cartoon marketing strategies, she would continue to remain at the helm of her company through the 1970s and into the 1980s. There were a few flare-ups of controversy as the new decade got under way.

On United Nations Day, held at New York's City Hall in 1965, Madame was honored for presenting a display of her International Dolls.

The feminist movement was gaining steam, and the doll industry was attacked as promoting stereotypical, oppressive ideals. News reporters covering the charges went to the Queen of American dollmakers for her take on the accusations. Never afraid to speak her mind, Madame Alexander took on Gloria Steinem, Germaine Greer and Betty Friedan. She countered that if playing with dolls was a precursor to female servitude, then how did they explain little boys who reached for their sisters' dolls, or requested dolls of their very own. In the *Peoria*

"Madame Alexander was the original feminist," asserts her longtime personal secretary Frances Einhorn.

Journal, Madame stated "indignantly" that "it is ridiculous to say that a doll makes a little girl have a false image of herself. What a doll does for a little girl is develop her capacity to love others and herself." She silenced their allegations with a blend of chutzpah and common sense. If only those loud, angry, young women had taken a moment to realize who they were assaulting. "Madame Alexander was *the* original feminist," personal secretary Frances Einhorn insists. "She was doing a man's job when the world was not always accepting or approving of an independent woman." Yes, if only the women-libbers had been privy to some of Madame's early days when she

Madame had a great appreciation and love for rare antiques and decorative art objects, which graced her home.

counseled her seamstresses and female laborers to be sensible and accountable for themselves. "She would often bring her favorite girls, the best workers, to Margaret Sanger's clinic for checkups and birth-control advice," daughter Mildred Behrman Birnbaum reveals. What an image: the controversial planned-parenthood crusader shaking hands with the dainty diminutive doll-maker—only in America!

Greeting the Bicentennial with the patriotic fervor that was so passé in the prior decade, Madame introduced the first six dolls of her First Ladies, or Presidents' Wives, series in 1976. This first 14-inch set depicted

early First Ladies, including Martha Washington, Abigail Adams and Dolley Madison. The dolls wore ensembles based painstakingly upon the actual inaugural gowns. Each release in the First Ladies series was anxiously awaited and purchased. They were undeniable hits, and these erstwhile dolls eventually had a fifteen-minute brush with sitcom fame in the 1990s on the CBS comedy *Murphy Brown*. Corky Sherwood, the beauty contestant turned anchorwoman, decorated her office with the Madame's presidential wives, and she would often interrupt her news coverage to see if any more First Ladies were being advertised in the doll publications.

Madame eventually created six sets of First Ladies; the final set was introduced in 1989-90. She believed in honoring those who helped build the country where her dreams had come true.

Maintaining the Legacy

The 1980s were filled with even more fame and fortune for Madame Alexander. There was an insistent demand for anything and everything Alexander. "The company had, and still has, the reputation of being sold in the quote 'better stores,'" says A. Glenn Mandeville. "There was a certain *je ne sais quoi* about their dolls that the other doll and toy companies just didn't have. When it was learned, for example, that the Alexander Doll Company was going to reissue a Scarlett doll with a vinyl head around 1983, the message was spread: 'This doll was going to be hot.' So people started to head to the department stores in droves, and there just weren't enough Scarletts to go around." Mandeville believes that the topsy-turvy ratio of supply and demand that character-ized the early 1980s was not an intentional marketing ploy. Many critics of the company have alleged that the factory deliberately turned out a minimal amount of product to drive up the perceived desirability. William Birnbaum shrugs off these charges, saying, "we could only work so fast in a factory. We tried to keep up with customer demand."

Mandeville, likewise, dismisses any calculated corporate conspiracy. "I would say it was just an error in

The Alexander legacy was carried on by, below, from left: Mildred Behrman Birnbaum, Richard Birnbaum, Kathleen Blotney Birnbaum, Bill Birnbaum and Madame. Opposite page: Madame dances with Prince Charming at a Disney World celebration in the early 1980s.

judgment. I feel that the company assumed, and mistakenly so, that their typical customer was a dowager who brought her little grandchild to the department store and held her hand while the little girl pointed at the display cabinets and said, 'I want that one, and that one, and that one.'

"That pairing of grandma and grandchild made up maybe twenty percent of their customers. By the 1980s an enormous percentage of their customers were adult collectors. When a shipment of dolls came in, all of them would sell out. And the Alexander Doll Company feared that an entire generation was about to grow up without ever seeing a Madame Alexander doll displayed in a store. So, they began to set a limit of two dolls to a customer, in order to preserve the dolls and their rightful places in the 'better' stores. They weren't campaigning to make their dolls more collectible. In fact, you could argue just the reverse. They wanted to keep the dolls out of the hands of the

Madame enjoyed the company of well-known national figures such as Alexander Haig in March 1983, above, and Jean Kirkpatrick, below left,

adult collectors and maintain them in an elegant department-store setting for the children and the next generation of children."

Whatever the motivation, the end results were pandemonium, mass hysteria and subterfuge and trickery on the part of the collectors. "Store detectives followed people around," Mandeville recalls. "They were making sure that you only bought one or two examples of a select doll." Sylvia Varon, a longtime friend and associate of Madame's, who lectured with her husband, David, on the care and maintenance of an Alexander doll collection, recollects an in-store appearance she made in the early 1980s. "We were in Pizitz, a department store in Birmingham, Alabama, and the 21-inch Scarlett O'Hara doll in the green velvet gown was put on sale. The customers began to line up at nine o'clock in the morning, and each person was handed one ticket with one number on it. That guaranteed you could buy just one Scarlett. You had to show your driver's license or some other official form of identification at the cash register. People were desperate to go home

with more than one doll; they would lie, beg or even try to steal to get more than one Scarlett. It was truly amazing."

As she glided into her nineties, Madame enjoyed her widespread success. The Alexander Doll Company was in demand as the purveyors of quality playthings, wise investments and breathtaking merchandise. It was a common sentiment among shop owners that a healthy supply of Alexander dolls on the shelf equaled success. A very prominent department-store president at a trade-show gathering was heard to comment that a sure-fire recipe for profits was "more Waterford Crystal and more Madame Alexander." When Beatrice Alexander

Behrman approved the Keats-inspired company motto, "A thing of beauty is a joy forever," had she visualized that her doll firm would be thriving and flourishing after more than sixty years?

Throughout the 1980s, announcements of a personal appearance by Madame at a department store or a charitable event resulted in throngs of admirers clutching their dolls for personal autographing. When Disneyland and Walt Disney World were each built (in 1955 and 1973, respectively), Madame Alexander and her collectors became frequent special guests at the two theme parks. A November 14, 1983, letter from Walt Disney World special events management to Madame reports enthusiastically that "between 9 am and 9:15 am, 3,100 attempted phone calls were

made for tickets to the Madame Alexander dinner. Every fifteen minutes after that, 630 attempted phone calls were made. Sue [who was fielding the calls] told me that you were more popular than Elvis."

"To this day, there is a plaque at the market square of Disney World reporting that the two times Madame Alexander had been there, the attendance was never equaled," Mandeville says. "People came out to see her and to touch her because of the Easter Bunny/Santa Claus connection," he theorizes. "There's a whole group of people who really do believe that Madame painted each little doll and drove each little nail into each doll's shoe. There really was a hero worship about her."

Personal secretary Miss Frances also recalls a special bond between Madame and her crowds of admir-

At a 1985 benefit dinner in Florida, Madame and Senator Bob Dole were all smiles.

THE WHITE HOUSE

February 7, 1985

Dear Madame Bea:

I'm delighted to join with your many friends in honoring you on this special day!

For generations, people world-wide, young and old, have delighted in your dolls. Through them, they have learned not only about other cultures but their own heritage as well.

On this your ninetieth birthday, I send my heartfelt congratulations. May your cherished memories be a happy reflection of the fullness of your life and the pleasure you have brought to so many.

Sincerely,

Nancy Reagan

Madame Bea Alexander
Ninetieth Birthday Dinner
Palm Beach, Florida

she still cared deeply about the company and its future, but her day-to-day involvement was certainly waning. Her friends report that she was understandably choosing to spend more and more time at her Palm Beach, Florida, home. She was supervising and advising, as opposed to minutely managing and designing.

With the creation of the Alexander Doll Company's first exclusive doll for The Enchanted Doll House in Manchester, Vermont, in 1980, the shop-exclusives and show-specials frenzy began. The Enchanted Doll was an 8-inch brunette dressed in the shop's pink-checked logo costume and was limited to 3,000 pieces. Later in the decade, when Collectors United (C.U.) asked the Alexander Doll Company to create their 1988 souvenir doll, the company adapted a doll that was part of its regular 8-inch hard-plastic collection to be Tippi, a portrait doll of Tippi Green, the daughter of C.U. founder Gary Green. According to A. Glenn Mandeville, Tippi, with a black ribbon around its neck, was limited to only 800 pieces, one of the first dolls to be released for an event in such a small quantity. "Collectors went berserk for that doll. It was just the perfect blending of all the elements," Mandeville recalls. "The doll was a ballerina dressed all in white, and it was the depiction of a beautiful Southern lady. The Green family was very well respected in the doll field, and the Tippi doll was the pinnacle of style and grace. The Alexander Doll Company had done special dolls in the past, but it was the Tippi doll that became

ers. "She moved people. I remember at Disney World a woman came up and touched the hem of Madame's dress. Madame was up on a platform, and this woman started to weep and then kissed the hem of the gown. She brought the dress to her lips, and actually kissed it. There was a fanaticism, like what you would see with Elvis and the Beatles, among her fans. They loved her and they were loyal to her."

In 1986 *Doll Reader* magazine recognized Madame with their 1986 Lifetime Achievement Award, and FAO Schwarz named her the First Lady of Dolls, in acknowledgment of her more than fifty years of doll sales at the store. Madame was ninety-one years old, and the yardstick by which everything else was measured. It's really the doll that brought the business into the 1990s."

Like a great showman who is aware of the perfect entrance and exit, Madame officially bid farewell to the world of doll-making in 1988. In many interviews during the late 1970s, Madame had expressed the hope that her great-grand-daughter, Stephanie, would make her way into the doll firm. She proudly spoke of Stephanie as an exceptional artist, a musician who plays both violin and piano, a talented writer and an exceptional equestrienne. She would also slyly add that her great-granddaughter looked just like her, a crafty tact that always forced the journalist to pay her and her great-grandchild a full-blown compliment. However, Stephanie Birnbaum's ascension into the family organization never occurred. Madame sold the

Like a great showman who is aware of the perfect entrance and exit, Madame officially bid farewell to the world of dollmaking in 1988.

family company to three private investors. She had great faith in these gentlemen. "They have a soul and a mind, and that is why I decided to sell the company to them," she told *Dolls* magazine in a telephone interview printed in the May/June 1988 issue. Though she knew they were not doll connoisseurs or artists, she believed that they were sincere.

Many Alexander collectors, however, believe that the firm lost its way between 1988 and 1995, as far as business management is concerned. The new owners insisted that Madame was active as a design consultant, but in reality, she was involved only on paper, a fabled figure-head. Her faltering health, combined with her Florida address, kept her out of the daily creative loop.

Even without their spiritual and artistic leader, designers at the Alexander Doll Company continued to try new outlets and enterprises, and produced many creatively successful and award-winning dolls. Twenty-one-inch porcelain dolls such as Carnival in

THE CITY OF NEW YORK
OFFICE OF THE MAYOR
NEW YORK, N.Y. 10007

April 20, 1988

Madame Alexander
President
Alexander Doll Company
615 West 131st Street
New York, New York

Dear Mme. Alexander:

Congratulations on the 65th Anniversary of the Alexander Doll Company and on your achievements as its founder and president.

New York is proud that one of America's most prestigious and enduring doll manufacturing companies was founded and continues to thrive here in our city, bringing joy to millions around the world.

When I'm 93, I hope I too will be as industrious and as creative a contributor to this city as you are.

With warmest regards,

Sincerely,

Edward I. Koch
Mayor

In 1988 the Alexander Doll Company celebrated its sixty-fifth anniversary. New York City's Mayor Ed Koch congratulated Madame with a warm letter, recognizing the doll manufacturer's long-time contribution to New York City.

Rio and Bride were released, in editions of 2,500 each, in 1989, with the goal of expanding the regular line and competing with the porcelain dolls that had become so popular among collectors. In 1991 the company was awarded a *Dolls* magazine Award of Excellence for the 21-inch porcelain Scarlett, followed by one in 1992 for the porcelain Thumbelina and Her Lady. Also in 1991, the popular 8-inch Wizard of Oz collection was introduced. This collection still thrives today and new characters are being added annually.

In 1990, the new owners attempted to further expand the business with another new venture, an association with the well-known German artist Hildegard Günzel. Günzel introduced a line of porcelain and vinyl dolls for the company that depicted children of different ethnic backgrounds. Her 1990 line netted several nominations for the DOTY (Doll of the Year) award and the *Dolls* magazine Award of Excellence; in 1992 her porcelain Courtney and Friends won a *Dolls* Award of Excellence. Another well-respected doll artist found her way into the Alexander fold in the 1990s. Robin Woods, working under the name of Alice Darling, joined the company in 1992 and introduced the Let's Play Dolls line, reflecting the company's attempt to further deepen their involvement in the play-doll business. Woods' dolls also brought numerous award nominations to the company. In spite of good intentions on the part of the new management and the artists involved, both of these associations ended by 1995.

The era of the late 1980s and early 1990s is considered particularly noteworthy for the many specially commissioned designs created by the company. Collectors' clubs, specialty shops and the Walt Disney World Teddy Bear & Doll Convention sought the services of the Alexander Doll Company to create exclusive souvenirs and limited editions. Disney World's competitive auction, a high point of the convention itinerary, always challenged the Alexander designers to dream up fantastical, opulent pieces. In 1993, a one-of-a-kind wedding tableau featuring 21-inch Cissy and two 8-inch attendants was auctioned off for $6,000 at Disneyland's Teddy Bear and Doll Classic while later

For the 1993 Walt Disney World Teddy Bear & Doll Convention, the Alexander Doll Company created a one-of-a-kind auction piece re-creating Claude Monet's *Women in the Garden* painting. The four-doll vignette brought $6,500.

that year, at Disney World's convention, a one-of-a-kind re-creation of Claude Monet's painting *Women in the Garden* was hammered down for $6,500.

Despite acquiring Madame's impeccable track record and her compelling mystique among her flock of loyal fans, the once-bright organization was steadily darkened by poor business management. By 1994 it teetered on the brink of financial ruin.

In 1995 the Alexander Doll Company was acquired

"Our history...contains an inherent challenge to live up to the standards of the past," says chairman Herbert Brown.

by the Kaizen Breakthrough Partnership, a private capital fund managed by Gefinor Acquisition Partners and sponsored by Gefinor, an international merchant banking group. Today, the company is thriving under this new 1990s arrangement. The new owners and their staff of designers, costumers, marketers and sales force have pledged to uphold Madame's place in the tapestry of twentieth-century America. In an October 1997 interview with *Dolls* magazine, current Alexander CEO and Chairman Herbert Brown confronted the company's seeming separation from Madame's original philosophy. "Back in 1923, when Madame founded this company, she had a mission in mind to produce dolls that could be played with and were helpful in a child's psychological and educational development. Actually, we became a collectible company not by design, but by default."

Brown went on to explain that he and his firm are in the business of making memories that are passed down from family member to family member, and that he planned on promoting the pure play-doll with as much gusto as the dolls that are pointed toward the mature collector. "Our history...contains an inherent challenge to live up to the standards of the past," he added. At the same time, he affirmed his company's commitment to "competing in an explosive, dynamic marketplace. After all," he pointed out,

The regal Rose Splendor, a 16-inch vinyl doll, was created as a 75th Anniversary limited edition in late 1998.

"Madame wouldn't sit idly by watching her competitors carve out piece after piece of the market. She would adapt and lead."

True to his word, Brown and his employees spent their first few years studying the Alexander archives and deciding which familiar faces to revive and revamp. The Little Women Journals™ play dolls introduced in 1997 were a blending of hands-on wardrobe play with juvenile reading and after-school activities. In 1998 a March sisters' *Midsummer Night's Dream* theater set was introduced that seemed to hearken back to the Tony Sarg mari-

In 1998 the Alexander Doll Company reintroduced porcelain dolls, including 15-inch Porcelain Margaret, a reinterpretation of the Margaret doll from the 1940s.

onette sets of the 1930s. A. Glenn Mandeville brands the Little Women Journals dolls a success: "The collection crosses the generations. It's aimed at the children but it's made so handsomely that the adult collector can't resist it, either. Plus, the Susan Sarandon and Winona Ryder movie has helped to make Little Women popular and contemporary once again."

The Alexander designers are honoring Madame's credo that dolls should be conduits to culture and the "finer things in life." They continue to pepper their yearly fare with salutes to famous art masterpieces, prima ballerina roles and children's literary classics.

The Cissy that re-emerged in 1996, with an assort-

ment of "Madame Alexander Couture" clothing, was most decidedly a grown-up doll, intended for the adult collector. The "New Girl in Town," as a doll magazine tagged her, was much more flamboyant and sensual than the original Cissy. "She is the true star of their line today," authority Mandeville asserts. "People are infatuated with her clothing and her sense of style. She fills the doll collector's vicarious need to be glamorous. People love all those exotic touches of star power." Indeed, in 1998, Cissy Barcelona, in black lace and a beaded shawl, received a Doll of the Year award.

The company is continuing its association with Disney World and its highly regarded Teddy Bear & Doll Convention. In 1996, Disney auction history was

In 1996 the Alexander Doll Company created a one-of-a-kind thirty-doll Alice in Wonderland chess set for the Walt Disney World Teddy Bear & Doll Convention auction. The set brought $42,000.

In the last decade of her life, Madame sparkled and glowed. Not only had she made her dreams come true, she had shared those dreams with children everywhere.

made when at the ninth annual Florida event, Florida collector Judene Hansen made a winning bid of $42,000 for the Alexander Doll Company's whimsical and breathtaking creation: a one-of-a-kind thirty-doll Alice in Wonderland Chess Set.

When the Alexander Doll Company celebrated its seventy-fifth anniversary in 1998, the creative team dreamed up new designs, such as the well-received Coca-Cola® Celebrates American Aviation; the Princess Diana Birthday Commemorative doll; the Harley-Davidson® Cissette; the glamorous 75th-Anniversary dolls like 21-inch Diamond Beauty, 16-inch Rose Splendor and 10-inch Pearl of the Twenties;

a 75th-Anniversary 8-inch Wendy and a 75th-Anniversary Huggable Huggums baby. They also put new spins on old favorites, reiussing popular dolls like the Dionne Quintuplets and their festive carousel, and Marybel Gets Well. Late in 1998 the company reintroduced porcelain with the new 16-inch Catherine and 15-inch Margaret dolls.

Madame Beatrice Alexander Behrman may have passed away on October 3, 1990, but her legacy, her vision and her accomplishments continue to thrive and grow. She is a true American original, a self-made woman from humble beginnings, who witnessed all her dreams come true through fierce determination and indomitable desire. Madame Alexander will not be forgotten as long as children laugh and mothers love, as long as little girls reach for their dolls in the middle of pitch-dark nights to confide just one more secret, and to share just one more whispered tale.

Part 2

The Dolls

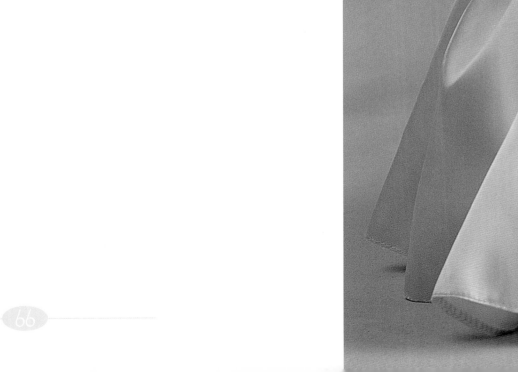

Literature

The novels of Beatrice Alexander's childhood left their impressions on the blossoming doll-maker. Among the very first dolls she ever created was a cloth homage to Lewis Carroll's *Alice's Adventures in Wonderland*. The March sisters of *Little Women* were recurring characters throughout Madame's doll-designing career, as were the protagonists from Charles Dickens', Kate Greenaway's and Shakespeare's works.

Maintaining her love of language throughout her whole life, Beatrice was captivated by the great American novel *Gone With the Wind* when it debuted in 1936. Scarlett and the other characters from this Southern epic are among the Alexander Doll Company's most beloved offerings.

In addition to creating dolls that would become life-long playmates and confidantes, Beatrice sought to have her children and their parents take inspiration from her creations. She hoped to open their minds. "A young girl should be able to learn from her dolls," Madame told interviewers time and again. "They should introduce her to the finer things in life, and she will be made a better person."

Dolls as three-dimensional messengers of fine writing and beautiful words have continued to be a staple of the Alexander Doll Company. From residents of Peter Pan's Never-Neverland to fairy-tale princes and princesses from Storyland, the legacy of Madame Alexander continues to weave the connection between the printed page and the collector's ability to dream.

Below: Scarletts, from left: 14 inches, composition, 1941-42; three 11-inch Scarletts, composition, 1940-43
Opposite page: Wendy; Peter Pan; each 15 inches, hard plastic, 1953-54

Little Women

Opposite page: Little Women set, from back: Laurie, 1987-92; Jo, 1991-92; Beth, 1991-92; Amy, 1991-92; Marmee, 1991-92; Meg, 1991-92; each 8 inches, hard plastic

Above: Little Women set, from left: Jo; Amy; Laurie; Meg; Beth; Marmee; each 12 inches, vinyl, 1989

Left: Little Women, each 16 inches, cloth, 1930-36

Above: Alexanderkins
Little Women, from left:
Meg; Amy; Beth; Jo;
Marmee; each 8 inches,
hard plastic, 1956

Left: Jo's World (bed-
room set and trunk)
from the Little Women
Journals™ collection,
with Little Women,
from left: Amy; Beth;
Meg; Jo; each 16 inches,
vinyl, 1997

Right: Little Women
stage set for A
Midsummer Night's
Dream, 38 1/2 inches
wide x 25 1/2 inches
high, with Little Women
dolls costumed as
Titania, Bottom and
Peaseblossom, 1998

Scarletts

Above: Alexanderkin Scarletts, each 8 inches, hard plastic; from left: 1955; 1955; 1965

Left: Alexanderkins, from left: Scarlett; Cousin Grace; each 8 inches, hard plastic, 1957

Following pages, from left: Coco Scarlett, 21 inches, vinyl, 1966; Coco Melanie, 21 inches, vinyl, 1966; Cissy Scarlett, 21 inches, hard plastic and vinyl, circa 1961; Elise Scarlett, 17 inches, hard plastic and vinyl, 1963; Cissy Melanie, 21 inches, hard plastic and vinyl, 1961

Left: Alexander-
kins, from left:
Scarlett; Melanie;
Cousin Karen;
each 8 inches,
hard plastic, 1956

Below: Scarlett
Jubilee set, from
left: Scarlett;
Mammy; Rhett;
each 8 inches,
hard plastic, 1989
only; Scarlett, 8
inches, hard plas-
tic, 1993 only

Left: Alexander-
kins, from left:
Aunt Agatha;
Aunt Pitty Pat;
each 8 inches,
hard plastic, 1957
Below: Scarlett,
21 inches, vinyl,
1989 only

Left: Scarlett,
21 inches, porcelain,
1991 only

Below: Scarlett
Hoop-Petti; Mam-
my; each 10 inches,
hard plastic, 1996

McGuffey Anas

Above: McGuffey Anas, each 16 inches, composition, 1937-44

Right: McGuffey Ana, with Lissy face, 11 1/2 inches, hard plastic, 1963

Opposite page: McGuffey Ana, 18 inches, hard plastic, 1948

Left: McGuffey Anas, from left: 21 inches, hard plastic 1948; 18 inches, hard plastic and vinyl, 1956

Below: McGuffey Anas, each 9 inches, composition, 1935-39

Right: Alexanderkin
McGuffey Ana, 8 inch-
es, hard plastic, 1956

Below, from left:
McGuffey Ana, 1948;
Alice in Wonderland,
1951 FAO Schwarz
exclusive; each 14 inches,
hard plastic

Heroes and Heroines

Above, from left:
Snow White, 1952;
Cinderella, 1950;
Prince Charming,
1950; each 14 inches,
hard plastic

Left: Ophelia;
Hamlet; each 12
inches, hard plastic,
1993 only

Above:
Alexanderkins:
Juliet; Romeo;
each 8 inches,
hard plastic, 1955

Right: Romeo;
Juliet; each 8 inch-
es, hard plastic,
1994 only

Top: Peter Pan set, from left: Captain Hook, 1992-93; Smee, 1993-94; Tiger Lily, 1992-93; John, 1993 only; Michael, 1992-93; Wendy, 1991-94; Peter Pan, 1991-94; Tinker Bell, 1991-present, each 8 inches; Mrs. Darling, 1993-94, 10 inches; each hard plastic; Nana, 6 inches, cloth, 1993 only

Above: Alexanderkin Tinker Bell, 8 inches, hard plastic, 1972

Left: Alexanderkins, from left: Alice in Wonderland, 1954; Peter Pan, 1953-54; Cinderella, 1954; each 8 inches, hard plastic

Opposite page: Cinderella, 21 inches, hard plastic, 1950

Left, from left: Kate Greenaway, 16 inches, cloth, 1936-38; Little Shaver, 22 inches, cloth, 1940-44; Little Lord Fauntleroy, 16 inches, cloth, circa 1932; Little Shaver, 7 inches, cloth, 1940-44

Below, from left: Rebecca of Sunnybrook Farm, 1996 only; Miss Muffet, 1965-88; Huckleberry Finn, 1989-91; Jack and Jill, 1987-90; each 8 inches, hard plastic

Above: Alice in
Wonderland set from
left: Tweedledum and
Tweedledee, 1998; Red
Queen; White King;
Knave; Humpty
Dumpty, each 1996;
Dormouse, 1998; Alice
in Wonderland, 1996;
Cheshire Cat, 1996;
each 8 inches,
hard plastic

Right, from left: Snow
White, 13 inches, com-
position, 1938; Dopey,
12 inches, composition,
1938; Dopey marionette
by Tony Sarg, 8 inches,
composition, circa 1936

Above: Kate Greenaways, from left: 14 inches; 16 inches; each composition, circa 1940

Left: Rebecca, from Daphne Du Maurier novel of the same name, 17 inches, composition, 1940

Below: Queen of Hearts (with hedgehog and flamingo), 10 inches, hard plastic, 1992; Alice and the White Rabbit, 10 inches, hard plastic, 1991; Tweedledee and Tweedledum; 8 inches each, hard plastic, 1994

Above: Brenda
Starr, each 12 inches,
vinyl, 1964

Above right: Nancy
Drew, 12 inches,
vinyl, 1967

Right: Sleeping
Beauty, 9 inches,
hard plastic, 1959

Above, front row, from left: Robin Hood, 1988-90; Maid Marion, 1989-91; Puss in Boots, 1995; Pollyanna, 1992-93; Little Thumbkins, 1995 only; back row, from left: The Red Shoes, 1995 only; Goldilocks, 1990-91; Bo Peep, 1962-85; The Snow Queen, 1995 only; each 8 inches, hard plastic

Left: Maid Marion, 21 inches, vinyl, 1992-93

Below: Anna Karenina, 10 inches, hard plastic, 1998

Opposite page: Maid Marion, 21 inches, vinyl, 1992-93

Left: Cinderella, 10 inches, hard plastic, 1989

Below, front row, from left: Hansel and Gretel, 1966-86; Curly Locks, 1987-88; Pinocchio, 1992-94; back row, from left: Queen of Hearts; 1987-90; Ladybird, 1988-89; Little Red Riding Hood, 1962-86; McGuffey Ana, 1965 only; each 8 inches, hard plastic

Above, from left: Heidi, 1997; Mary Lennox, 1997; Gigi, 1998, each 8 inches, hard plastic

Right and opposite page: Anna Karenina Trunk Set dolls, 10 inches, hard plastic, 1998

Below, from left: Fairy Godmother, 1997; Poor Cinderella, 1997; Cinderella, 1995; each 8 inches; Really Ugly Stepsister, 10 inches, 1997; Ugly Stepsister, 8 inches, 1997; each hard plastic

Above, from left: Little Red Riding Hood, 1991; Snow White, 1995; Anne of Green Gables, 1997; Mary Had a Little Lamb, 1996; each 8 inches, hard plastic

Opposite page, above right, from left: Hickory, Dickory Dock, 1998; Mother Goose, 1997; Rapunzel, 1995; each 8 inches, hard plastic

Right, from left: Fairy of Virtue; Fairy of Song; Sleeping Beauty; Fairy of Beauty; each 8 inches, hard plastic, 1997

Cinema and Television

It is only fitting that Madame Alexander, the leading lady of the doll world, should have saluted the leading ladies of Tinseltown. Throughout the Alexander Doll Company's history, charismatic, crowd-pleasing actresses whose images flickered across the American landscape have been lovingly translated into doll form. In earlier decades, Katharine Hepburn, Elizabeth Taylor, Mary Martin and Lucille Ball were just some of the big-screen talents that were impressively scaled down to doll size. And, of course, there was Margaret O'Brien, a pint-sized actress whose talent and box-office clout were colossal.

When doll fanciers bought one of Madame's movie-star homages, they held a little bit of Hollywood in their hands. Glamour and sophistication were magically transformed into palm-size plastic icons. As gathering around the television set became a national fixation, the Alexander Doll Company naturally tuned into the luminaries who were stars of our living rooms. *That Girl*'s Marlo Thomas, Carolyn Jones of *The Addams Family*, and Shari Lewis are just a few of the weekly-episodic women who have been honored with meticulously crafted likenesses. These legendary silver-screen and small-screen dolls may stand no higher than two feet, but their potency and popularity are immeasurable.

Left, from left: Mary Martin, 14 inches, hard plastic, 1948-50; two Margaret O'Brien dolls, each 14 inches, hard plastic, 1947

Opposite: The Sound of Music set, clockwise from Maria, 17 inches; Liesl, 14 inches; Marta, 11 inches; Gretl, 11 inches; Louisa, 14 inches; Brigitta, 14 inches; Friedrich, 11 inches, vinyl, 1965-70

Above: Walt Disney's Sleeping Beauty, 17 inches, hard plastic and vinyl, 1959

Above: The Story Princess from television's *The Howdy Doody Show*, 8 inches, hard plastic, 1956

Right: Katharine Hepburn as Eva Lovelace in the movie *Morning Glory*, 23 inches, cloth, 1934

Above, from left: Margaret O'Brien, 18 inches, hard plastic, 1947; Mary Martin, 18 inches, hard plastic, 1948-50; Annabelle, 18 inches, hard plastic, 1952

Right and opposite page:
Lucille Ball as a bride in
the movie *Forever
Darling*, 20 inches, hard
plastic and vinyl, 1956

Below, from left:
Mouseketeer, 1991 only;
Mouseketeer prototype,
1991; Roundup Day
Mouseketeer,
1992; each 8 inches,
hard plastic

Opposite page, top: The Wizard of Oz™ set, from left: Glinda the Good Witch, 1992-95; Auntie Em, 1995 only; Emerald City Dorothy, 1994 only; Toto, 1997 only; Lullaby Munchkin, 1995 only; each 8 inches, hard plastic

Left: The Wizard of Oz™ set, 1998, with There's No Place Like Home Dollhouse, 1997, and, from left: Miss Gulch, 10 inches, 1997, with bicycle and Toto; The Wicked Witch of the West, 10 inches, 1997; The Tin Man, 8 inches, 1993; The Wizard, 8 inches, 1998, with State Fair Balloon; The Cowardly Lion, 8 inches, 1993; The Scarecrow, 8 inches, 1993; Dorothy with Toto, 8 inches, 1991; Glinda the Good Witch, 10 inches, 1997; each hard plastic

Above: The Wizard of Oz™ set, from left: The Wicked Witch of the West, Winged Monkey, The Wizard of Oz, each 1994 only; Munchkin Peasant, The Mayor of Munchkinland, Munchkin Herald, each 1994-95; Lollipop Munchkin, 1995 only; each 8 inches, hard plastic

Right, from left: Shari Lewis, 20 inches, hard plastic and vinyl, 1959; Marlo Thomas as television's *That Girl*, 17 inches, vinyl, 1967

Below: Showgirls, each 10 inches, hard plastic, 1996 only, limited edition of 950 for Madame Alexander Doll Club Convention

Above: Camelot set, from left: Guinevere, 8 inches; Morgan LeFay, 10 inches; Lancelot, 8 inches; each hard plastic, 1995 only

Left: The Sound of Music set, clockwise from Maria, 12 inches, vinyl; Brigitta, 10 inches; Louisa, 10 inches; Friedrich, 8 inches; Liesl, 10 inches; Gretl; 8 inches; Marta, 8 inches; each hard plastic, 1971-73

The Sound of Music™ set, from left: Kurt, 9 inches, 1998; Gretl, 8 inches, 1998; Maria's Travel
Ensemble, 10 inches, 1997; Louisa, 10 inches, 1998; Friedrich, 10 inches, 1998; Marta, 8 inches,
1998; Captain Von Trapp, 10 inches, 1998; Liesl, 10 inches, 1998; Maria at the Abbey, 10 inches,
1997; Mother Superior, 10 inches, 1997; Brigitta, 9 inches, 1998; each hard plastic
(The guitar belongs to Maria at the Abbey.)

Left, from back: Belle, from *Beauty and the Beast*, 8 inches, 1994 only; Mary Poppins, 10 inches, 1995 only; Snow White, 8 inches, 1972-76; each hard plastic

Opposite page: The Addams Family, from left: Pugsley, 8 inches; Thing in his black box; Morticia, 10 inches; Gomez, 10 inches; Wednesday, 8 inches; each hard plastic, 1997

Right: Little Women, from left, Meg; Beth; Jo; Amy; Marmee; each 14 inches, hard plastic, 1949. These dolls were made as replicas of the characters from the 1949 film *Little Women*.

Fine Arts

A love for all things classical and cultural always held a special place in Madame Alexander's soul. With her daughter, Mildred, by her side, the determined dollmaker would take time out from her relentless schedule to attend the world-famous Metropolitan Opera House. Together, mother and daughter were swept away by the arias of Verdi and the symphonies of Strauss. Mildred was actively encouraged by her mother to pursue a path of palettes and canvases and, indeed, grew up to be a well-regarded painter.

The Alexander Doll Company has always respected its founder's infatuation with the performing arts and the fine arts. Every year, at least one ballerina seemingly pirouettes from the pages of the company's catalog, and Madame's love of contraltos and sopranos has been embodied in salutes to Puccini's fragile, lyrical heroines, such as Mimi and Madame Butterfly. The visions of master painters as diverse as Renoir, Goya, Sargent and Gainsborough have lent themselves to doll re-creations. Madame's desire to reach beyond the confines of her poverty-ridden upbringing enabled her to raise dollmaking to a hitherto-unscaled plateau.

Below, from left: Thomas Gainsborough's Blue Boy; Sir Thomas Lawrence's Pinkie; each 8 inches, hard plastic, 1997
Opposite page: Giselle, 16 inches, vinyl, 1997

Above: Cissette ballerinas, from left: 1963; 1963; 1957; each 9 inches, hard plastic

Right: Ballerinas, from left: Tippi, 1988 only, limited edition of 800 for Collector's United Gathering; 1995 only; 1990-91; 1992-94; 1983 only, part of limited-production trunk set for The Enchanted Doll House, Manchester, Vermont; each 8 inches, hard plastic

Left: Alexanderkin
ballerinas, each
8 inches, hard
plastic, 1953
Below: Shadow
Madame Butterfly,
8 inches, hard
plastic, 1997

From left: Nina Ballerina, 21 inches, 1951; Nina Ballerina, 21 inches, 1948; Karen
Ballerina, 14 inches, 1947-48; Karen Ballerina, 18 inches, 1947-48; Nina Ballerina, 14
inches, 1948; Treena Ballerina, 18 inches, 1951; each hard plastic

Opposite page, far left: Lilac Fairie Ballerina, 21 inches, vinyl, 1993-1994

Left, from left: Renoir, 21 inches, vinyl, 1965; Goya, 21 inches, vinyl, 1968

Opposite page, bottom left: Fine Arts Collection, from left: Renoir, 1967-68; Degas Girl, 1967-87; Sargent, 1984-85; Ingres, 1987 only; Manet, 1986-87; each 14 inches, vinyl

Below, from left: Giselle, 16 inches, vinyl, 1997; Wendy Ballerina, 8 inches; hard plastic, 1997; Swan Lake, 16 inches, vinyl, 1997; Degas' Ballerina, 10 inches, hard plastic; 1998; The Nutcracker, 16 inches, vinyl, 1998

Fashions of Earlier Eras

Growing up over her father's doll hospital, young Beatrice Alexander was impressed by the rich clothing worn by New York's "carriage trade," who would arrive at her door in velvet cloaks and boasting ornately plumed hats. "I vowed I would have a carriage and those feathers!" Madame often recalled. And, indeed, the little girl from the Lower East Side did grow up to have an impeccable wardrobe and an elegant lifestyle.

Madame believed that clothing made the woman, and this philosophy was showcased in the well-groomed, well-heeled social butterflies she designed. The dolls that embody yesteryear's finery—such as The Godey Ladies, the Mystery Dolls and the Fashions of a Century, all from the late 1940s and early 1950s—are paeans to past perfection. And more recently, creations like the Flappers, Diamond Lil and other retro wonders continue in earnest. It has been said that Alexander dolls are draped in dreams. The splendid costumes of "days gone by" are testaments to the dreams of Madame Alexander, a visionary of vestments.

Below: Godey Ladies, each 14 inches, hard plastic, 1949
Opposite page: Mystery Doll Lady with Rhinestone Beauty Mark, 21 inches, hard plastic, 1951

Right: Madeline, 17 inches and 21 inches, composition, 1940

Below, from left: Lady Windermere; Orchard Princess; Godey Lady; each 21 inches, composition, 1946

Above: Alexanderkins,
from left: Little Victoria,
1954; The French
Flower Girl, 1956;
Apple Annie, 1953;
each 8 inches,
hard plastic

Left: Cissette Lady
Hamilton, 9 inches,
hard plastic, 1957

The nine dolls on these pages are from the group called Fashions of a Century. Each is 18 inches, hard plastic, 1951.

Left: Alexanderkins, from left: Southern Belle, 1953; Little Southern Girl, 1954; Southern Belle, 1954; each 8 inches, hard plastic

Right: Alexanderkins, from left: Garden Party, 1956; First Long Party Dress, 1957; Graduation, 1957; each 8 inches, hard plastic

Below: Alexanderkins Me and My Shadow Group, from left: Victoria; Mary Louise; Elaine; each 8 inches, hard plastic, 1954

Above: From the Me and My Shadow Series, from left: Elaine; Cheri; Agatha; each 18 inches, hard plastic, 1954

Left: From the Me and My Shadow Series, from left: Mary Louise; Victoria; each 18 inches, hard plastic, 1954

The Mystery Dolls, from left: Champs Elysee; Deborah Bride; Lady with
Rhinestone Beauty Mark; Deborah Ballerina; Kathryn Grayson; each 21 inches,
hard plastic, 1951. Not shown in picture is the sixth Mystery Doll, Arlene Dahl.

Opposite page:
Mystery Doll Champs
Elysee, 21 inches, hard
plastic, 1951

Right: Alexanderkins,
from left: Little Made-
line; Little Victoria;
Country Picnic;
each 8 inches,
hard plastic, 1953

Left: Alexanderkins,
from left: Godey Lady,
1955; Godey Lady, 1955;
Nana the Governess,
1957; each 8 inches,
hard plastic

Below: From the
Glamour Girl Walker
Series, from left: Civil
War; Edwardian; Vic-
torian; each 18 inches,
hard plastic, 1953

Above: Cissys, from
left: Very Sophisti-
cated Gown, from
Cissy Models Her
Formal Gowns series,
1957; Long Torso
Gown, from A
Child's Dream
Come True series,
1955; Long-stemmed
Look, from Cissy
Parade Series, 1956;
each 21 inches, hard
plastic and vinyl

Right, from left: Cissy
Godey, 21 inches,
hard plastic and vinyl;
Elise Godey Style, 17
inches, hard plastic
and vinyl; each 1962

Left, from left: Cissy Renoir, 21 inches, hard plastic and vinyl, 1961; Elise Renoir, 17 inches, hard plastic and vinyl, 1963; Cissy Godey, 21 inches, hard plastic and vinyl, 1961

Below: Cissettes, from left: Goldrush Girl, 1963; Gibson Girl, 1962; Gibson Girl, 1963; Klondike Kate, 1963; each 9 inches, hard plastic

Above, from left: The Southern Belle (Lissy), 1963; Lissy Graduate, 1957; each 11 1/2 inches, hard plastic

Right: Portrait Agatha, 21 inches, vinyl, 1975

Below: Cissette Flappers, from left: Blue Zircon (December), 1992; Black, 1988; Ruby (July), 1992; Sapphire (September), 1992; White, 1990-91; Red, 1988-89; Pearl (June), 1992; each 10 inches, hard plastic

Above: Portrette Cissettes, from left: Diamond Lil, 1993, limited edition of 876 for Madame Alexander Doll Club convention; Melinda, 1968; Agatha, 1968; Cameo Lady, 1991, limited edition of 1,000 for Collectors United in Georgia; each 10 inches, hard plastic

Left: Portrait Southern Belle, 21 inches, vinyl, 1965

Modern Fashions

Among the greatest highlights of Madame Alexander's career were surely the four times she was awarded the prestigious Fashion Academy's Gold Medal: 1951 through 1954. Winning against competition that included the highest-regarded fashion designers of the years, Madame was lauded for "reflecting the ultimate in design beauty, for encouraging good taste and clothes appreciation and for symbolizing 'best dressed' so perfectly."

With her usual foresight, Madame Alexander launched Cissy, the first full-figured fashion doll, in 1955, four years before another soon-to-be-legendary fashion doll arrived on the scene. With characteristic bravado, Madame heralded Cissy's arrival with this pronouncement: "She is the newest and most exciting doll in the world."

Hyperbole aside, Cissy and her diminutive cousin, 1957's 9-inch Cissette, embody every woman's desire to look spectacular and to turn heads. Refined and redesigned in 1996, today's Cissy and Cissette model clothing that captures the realities and fantasies of modern-day catwalks from Milan to Manhattan.

Below: Cissettes, from left: A Spectator Sports Outfit, 1958; Lace peplum dress, circa 1958; Tea in the Garden, 1958; each 9 inches, hard plastic

Opposite page: Cissy Milan, 21 inches, vinyl, 1998, limited edition of 1,500

Above: Cissettes, from
left: Gold Net Formal,
1961; Lace Gown,
1963; A Lovely Vision,
1959; each 9 inches,
hard plastic

Right: Cissettes, from
left: Afternoon Tea;
Day in the Village;
For Every Occasion;
each 9 inches, hard
plastic, 1958

Left: Cissettes, from left: Margot, A Vision to Behold, 1961; Margot, Looking Very Elegant, 1961; Cissette, Fitted Gown with a Regal Air, 1957; each 9 inches, hard plastic

Below: Cissettes, from left: Fuschia Sheath, 1963; The Junior League, 1957; Lace Dress for a Formal Occasion, 1959; Organdy and Lace, circa 1959; each 9 inches, hard plastic

Cissy Fashion Group, from left: Cissy Walks Her Dog, 1956; Cissy
Wears an Afternoon Dress, circa 1959; Cissy Wears a Smart Cocktail
Dress, 1956; Cissy, Ripples of Rhythm, 1957; Cissy Dressed for Any
Summer Morning, 1957; each 21 inches, hard plastic and vinyl

Right, from left:
COCA-COLA®
Carhop, 1997; Harley-
Davidson® Cissette,
1998; COCA-
COLA® Celebrates
American Aviation
1998; each 10 inches,
hard plastic

Below, from left: Cissy
Yellow Satin Gown,
from A Child's Dream
Come True series,
1956; Lady in Red,
from Dolls to
Remember series, 1958;
each hard plastic and
vinyl, 21 inches

Left: 75th Anniversary Diamond
Beauty, vinyl, 21 inches, 1998

Below: Coppertone® Beach Set,
8 inches, hard plastic, 1998;
Cissette Daisy Resort Ensemble
(both outfits), 10 inches, hard
plastic, 1998

From left: Cissy Gold Net Formal, 20 inches, circa 1959;
Elise Dance Gown, 17 inches, 1958; Elise Cornflower Blue
Formal Gown, 17 inches, 1960; Cissy Dance Gown,
20 inches, 1958; each hard plastic and vinyl

Opposite page: Cissy Café Rose, 21 inches, vinyl, 1996

Left: Cissette Dressed for the Theatre, 9 inches, hard plastic, 1957

Below: Cissy by Scassi, 21 inches, vinyl, 1990, limited production for FAO Schwarz in New York City; Cissy Café Rose, 21 inches, vinyl, 1996, limited edition of 2,500. Both Caucasian and African-American dolls were produced, but the African-American edition was very limited.

Left: Cissy's Secret Armoire, 21 inches, vinyl, 1997; Coco and Cleo Travel Abroad, 16 inches, vinyl, 1997

Opposite page, right: Cissettes, from left: Calla Lily, 1998; Onyx, 1997; Red Sequin, 1998; Tea Rose, 1998; Gardenia, 1998; Café Rose, 1997; each 10 inches, hard plastic

Above: Belle Epoque (both outfits), 16 inches, vinyl, 1998

Right: Cissy Barcelona (Caucasian and African American), two views, 21 inches, vinyl, 1998; each version limited to an edition of 1,500

Above: Cissy Paris,
21 inches, vinyl, 1998, limited edition of 1,500

American Children

Dolls should look like children, and children should look like dolls. That, in a nutshell, was Madame Alexander's philosophy for successful dollmaking. Since her own childhood years were more scrappy than idyllic, Madame delighted in imagining a world where children were encouraged to be carefree, light-hearted and young. The juvenile dolls that she created celebrate an American child's right to pursue happiness. Her young boy and girl dolls are testaments to well-nurtured upbringings, where a change of clothing keeps pace with a booked-up social calendar. Sample a few of her creations' names: Shopping Jaunt, Looking Especially Pretty, Apple Pie, Wendy Can Read, First Communion and Party Plaid.

The Alexander child doll is a tribute to the American culture in which children are revered, and are encouraged to learn and to worship without fear. As the social climate of the United States changed during the firm's first seventy-five years, the complexion of the Alexander children, likewise, altered and broadened. Non-white children joined the ranks of the tots who were always on the go, whether they were Dressed Like Mommy, singing in the Boys Choir of Harlem, or pretending to be firefighters and master chefs. Always created with youngsters in mind, some of the Alexander Doll Company's most beloved figures throughout the firm's history depict children themselves.

Below, from left: Kelly, 1959; Lissy, 1957-58; Lissy, 1956; each 11 1/2 inches, hard plastic
Opposite page: Alexanderkins: The Cherry Twins, 1957, each 8 inches, hard plastic

Right, from left: Pinky Baby, 20 inches, 1937; Slumbermate, 14 inches, 1940; each composition and cloth

Below, from left: Polly Pigtails, 1949-51; Kathy, 1949-51; Annabelle, 1952; each 14 inches, hard plastic

Above left: Cynthia, 18 inches, hard plastic, 1952

Above right: Twins, 12 inches, composition, 1936

Left: Alexanderkins, from left: Emerald Green Dress, White Pinafore, 1956; Favorite Outfit, 1953; Azalea Pink Dress, Pinafore; 1953-54; each 8 inches, hard plastic

Clockwise, from front: Polly Pigtails, 1990 limited edition for Madame Alexander Doll Club (MADC); Wendy, 1989, first limited edition for MADC; From the Madame's Sketchbook, 1997, limited edition of 1,500 for MADC; Wendy Joins MADC, 1995, limited edition of 1,500 for MADC; Wendy Loves Being Best Friends, 1993, limited edition for MADC; The Enchanted Doll, 1980, limited edition of 3,000 for The Enchanted Doll House in Manchester, Vermont; Springtime, 1991 limited edition of 1,600 for MADC Premiere attendees; Wendy's Best Friend Maggie, 1994, limited edition of 2,500 for MADC; each 8 inches, hard plastic

Above: Alexanderkins, from left: Gay as a Jonquil, 1959; Rosebud Print and Polished Cotton, 1956; First Communion, 1957; Rosebuds and Ribbons, 1957; each 8 inches, hard plastic

Left, from left: Sweet Tears, 14 inches, vinyl, 1965-82; Mary Cassatt Baby, 14 inches, vinyl and cloth; 1969-70; Kathy Cry Dolly, 11 inches, vinyl, 1957-58

Below: Alexanderkins, from left: Pink Gabardine Coat, 1953; Goes to the Matinee, 1955; So Dressed Up, 1954; A Charming Ensemble, 1956; each 8 inches, hard plastic

Above, from left: Kelly, 1959; Lissy "Separates," 1956; Lissy Organdy Pinafore, 1957; Lissy Summer Outfit, circa 1958; each 11 1/2 inches, hard plastic

Right: Alexanderkins, from left: The Sailor Girl, 1956; A-line Dress, 1965; Little Madeline, exclusive for Neiman-Marcus, 1954; each 8 inches, hard plastic

Left: Alexanderkins, from left: Summer Afternoon, 1956; Shopping Jaunt, 1956; Frilly Organdy Dress, Pinafore; 1953; each 8 inches, hard plastic

Above: Alexanderkins, from left: Dozens of Blossoms, 1957; Maggie Mix Up, 1961; Looking Especially Pretty, 1960; Dozens of Blossoms, 1957; each 8 inches, hard plastic

Left: Alexanderkins, from left: Littlest Kitten, 1963; Little Genius. 1956; Little Genius, 1956; each 8 inches, hard plastic

Opposite page, top: Muffins, from left: Birthday Party, 1989 only; White Dress, 1990 only; Party Plaid, 1990 only; Party Time, 1989 only; each 12 inches, vinyl

Left: Americana Collection, from left: Colonial Girl, 1962-70; Cowboy, 1967-69; Cowgirl, 1966-70; Miss USA, 1966-68; Betsy Ross, 1967-87; Eskimo, 1966-69; Hawaiian Girl, 1966-69; each 8 inches, hard plastic

Opposite page, bottom: Bobby Sox, 1990 only, exclusive to Disneyworld and Disneyland; Wendy's Favorite Pastime, 1994 only, exclusive to Disneyworld and Disneyland; Peppermint Twist, 1995 only; each 8 inches, hard plastic

Below: Alexanderkins, from left: The Most Fashionable Girl in Town, 1957; Organdy Party Dress, 1958; Wendy Can Read, 1957; each 8 inches, hard plastic

Right: Golf Girl and Boy, each 8 inches, hard plastic, 1997

Below: Mommy and Me on the Go, 8 inches and 10 inches, hard plastic, 1996

Above, from left: September, 1989 only; Apple Pie, 1991 only; April, 1990-91; Sweet Sixteen, 1991-92; Brooke, 1988 FAO Schwarz exclusive; each 14 inches, vinyl

Left: First Communion, 8 inches, hard plastic, 1995

Below: Dressed Like Mommy, 1995; Get Well, 1998; each 8 inches, hard plastic

Opposite page: Mop Top Wendy, 8 inches, hard plastic, 1994

Left: Mommy and Me at Home, 10 inches and 8 inches, hard plastic, 1996

Below: Park Avenue Wendy; Alex the Bellhop; each 8 inches, hard plastic, 1997

Right, from left: Congratulations, 1998; Happy Birthday Maggie, 1997; Thank You, 1997; each 8 inches, hard plastic

Below, from left: Wendy Makes it Special, 1997; Cake Top Bride and Groom, 1996; 75th Anniversary Wendy, 1998; each 8 inches, hard plastic

Top, from left: Huggums Pretty in Pink, 1997; Huggums Blue Check Denton (African American), 1997; Pink Stripe Huggums, 1998; each 12 inches, vinyl; Lifelike Baby Victoria, 18 inches, vinyl, 1998; Rainbow Huggums, 1998; Huggums Christening, 1996; each 12 inches, vinyl

Above, from left: Ice Skater, 1990-91; Cheerleader, 1992-93; All Star, 1993-94; Majorette, 1991-92; Scouting, 1991-92; each 8 inches, hard plastic

Above: Boys Choir of Harlem, 8 inches, hard plastic, 1996

Right: Marybel Gets Well, 15 inches, vinyl, originally introduced in 1959, reproduced in 1998

Below, from left: Fire Fighter Wendy, 1997; Chef Alex, 1997; Easter, 1996; Artiste Wendy, 1997; each 8 inches, hard plastic

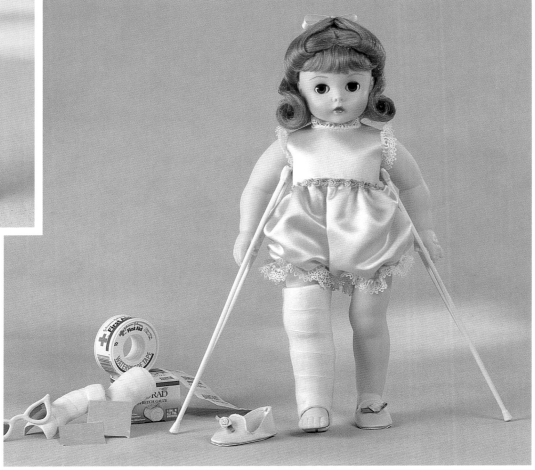

Left, from left: Ice Skating Girl; Soccer Girl, each 1997; Maggie Mix-Up, originally introduced in the 1960s and reproduced in honor of 1997 U. S. Postal Service commemorative stamp; each 8 inches, hard plastic

Below, from left: Blue Dupionne Kelly, 20 inches, vinyl, 1998; Yellow Ribbon Pussycat, 14 inches, vinyl, 1998; Kelly Blue Gingham, 20 inches, vinyl, 1997; White Floral Party Kelly, 15 inches, vinyl, 1998

Royalty and Celebrities

Madame Alexander's fascination with wealth and prestige is revealed most tellingly in her line of monarchical dolls. She was an admitted Anglophile, and her love and appreciation for pomp and circumstance were best displayed in her frequent tributes to Britain's royal Windsor family.

It is almost as if Madame had tucked away in her pastel business attire a barometer that measured the sales appeal of a front-page event. How else to explain, for example, her uncanny seizing of the licensing rights to the Dionne Quintuplets when news of their multiple birth broke in 1934? From heads of state to headliners, from Olympic athletes to running mates, the Alexander Doll Company honored the men and women who helped to forge the 20th century as we know it. Madame and her subsequent designers were savvy about converting real-life champions into blue-ribbon dolls.

Below, from left: Madame Alexander, 21 inches, vinyl, 1995, limited edition of 500 honoring Madame Alexander's 100th birthday; Madame Alexander, 21 inches, vinyl, 1984-87
Opposite page: Queen Elizabeth II, 20 inches, hard plastic and vinyl, circa 1960. Very few of these dolls using the "Sleeping Beauty" face were produced.

Right: Dionne Quintuplet, 16 inches, cloth, 1935-36

Below: The Dionne Quintuplets in the original stroller, from left: Cécile; Annette; Marie; Emilie; Yvonne; each 8 inches, composition, 1935-39

Above: The Dionne Quintuplets, from left: Yvonne; Cécile; Annette; Marie; Emilie; each 11 inches, composition, 1937-38

Left: The Dionne Quintuplets on their Carousel, clockwise from Cécile in green: Annette in yellow; Marie in blue; Yvonne in pink; Emilie in lilac; each 8 inches, hard plastic, first produced in 1935 and reproduced in 1998

Above: Three
Princess Elizabeths,
each 13 inches, com-
position, 1937-41

Right: Princess
Margaret Rose,
from left: 1947; 1948;
each 18 inches,
hard plastic

Above: Cissettes, from left:
Queen Elizabeth II, 1962;
Queen Elizabeth II, 1958;
Queen Elizabeth II, 1963;
each 9 inches, hard plastic

Left: Alexanderkins, from
left: Prince Charles;
Princess Anne; 8 inches,
hard plastic, 1957

Below: Alexanderkins, from
left,: Queen Elizabeth II, 1955;
Lady in Waiting, 1955; Queen
Elizabeth, 1954; each 8 inches,
hard plastic

From left: Lady Churchill; Queen Elizabeth II; Maid of
Honor; Maid of Honor; Princess Margaret Rose;
Maid of Honor; each 18 inches, hard plastic, 1953

Above: Queen Elizabeths, from left: Jacqueline face, 21 inches, vinyl, 1965; Cissy face, 21 inches, hard plastic and vinyl, 1955; Elise face, 17 inches, hard plastic and vinyl, 1963; Cissy face, 21 inches, hard plastic and vinyl, circa 1962

Right: Queen Elizabeth II, 20 inches, hard plastic and vinyl, circa 1960

Above, from left:
Lady Hamilton, 1968; Jenny Lind, 1969; each 21 inches, vinyl

Left: Jenny Lind, 10 inches, hard plastic, 1970 only

Below, from left: Queen Elizabeth II, 8 inches, hard plastic, 1992 only; Empress Elisabeth of Austria, 10 inches, hard plastic, 1991 only, for My Doll House in Virginia; Queen Elizabeth I, 10 inches, hard plastic, 1990 only, for My Doll House in Virginia; Queen, 10 inches, hard plastic, 1972-73

Opposite page: Babs Skaters, from left: 21 inches; 14 inches; each hard plastic, 1947

Left: Babs Skaters, from left: 1948; 1949-50; each 14 inches, hard plastic

Below: Babs Skaters, from left: 1949-50; 1948-49; each 18 inches, hard plastic.

These were inspired by Barbara Ann Scott, an Olympic figure skater of the late 1940s.

Above: Cissette Jacquelines, each 9 inches, hard plastic, 1962

Right: Jacqueline in inaugural gown, 21 inches, vinyl, 1961

Left: Cissette Jacquelines, each 9 inches, hard plastic, 1962

Below, from left: Shadow Jackie Suit; Shadow Jackie Opera Coat/ Evening Dress; Shadow Jackie Beaded Cocktail Dress; each 10 inches, hard plastic, 1997

Left, from left: Christopher Columbus; Queen Isabella; each 8 inches, hard plastic, 1992

Below: First Ladies set VI, from left: Mamie Eisenhower; Lou Hoover; Eleanor Roosevelt; Bess Truman; Jackie Kennedy; Grace Coolidge; each 14 inches, vinyl, 1989-90

Left: Shadow Polka
Dot Lucy, 10 inches,
hard plastic, 1998

Brides and Bridal Parties

Despite her pioneering independence and business drive, Madame Alexander was a traditionalist at heart. She especially loved the drama and the time-honored customs that surround a wedding and adored designing breathtaking fantasy wear for this most sacred ceremony. It's a well-known truism that on her wedding day every bride is beautiful, and the Alexander bridal dolls, with their handsome and lovely attendants, convey the joy of a shared life about to begin.

The Alexander Doll Company has cast its most beloved heroines in the role of radiant wife-to-be.

Cissy, Cissette, Elise and the Alexanderkins have all strolled down the flower-strewn nuptial aisle. As decades pass, and social mores relax and are then redefined, the Alexander bride dolls continue to be popular with children, collectors and women entering into the bonds of matrimony. After all, who wants a Jacqueline-faced bride doll? Be quiet and you can hear the collectors cry, "I do."

Below: Cissette Bridesmaids, from left: 1959; 1958; 1957; each 9 inches, hard plastic
Opposite page: Pink Bride, 21 inches, hard plastic, 1950

Above, from left: Lucy
Bride; 21 inches,
hard plastic, 1949;
Bride, 21 inches,
hard plastic, 1950

Right, from left:
Godey Man; Godey
Bride; each 14 inches,
hard plastic, 1949

Left: Pink Brides, from
left: 21 inches; 18 inches
each hard plastic, 1950

Below: Rosamund
Bridesmaid, 18 inches,
hard plastic, 1951-52

Opposite page:
Margaret Rose
Bridesmaid,
21 inches, hard
plastic, 1950

Left: Cissette
Brides, from left:
1957; 1958; 1959;
each 9 inches,
hard plastic

Right: Alexanderkins,
from left: Bridesmaid,
1955; Flower Girl,
1956; Bride, 1953-54;
Groom, 1953; The
Best Man, 1955; each
8 inches, hard plastic

Below: Alexanderkins,
from left: Pink Bride,
1959; Groom, 1956;
Bride, 1964, each 8
inches, hard plastic

The Bridal Group, from left: Ringbearer, 12 inches, 1950; Groom, 21 inches, 1950; Peggy Bride, 21 inches, 1950; Flower Girl, 14 inches, 1954; Margaret Rose Bridesmaids, brunette and blond, each 21 inches, 1950; each hard plastic

Above:
Alexanderkins,
from left:
Bridesmaid, 1956;
Bridesmaid, 1957;
Flower Girl, 1957;
each 8 inches,
hard plastic

Right, from left:
Bridesmaid,
8 inches, hard
plastic; 1953; Lissy
Bride, 11 1/2 inches,
hard plastic, 1958

Opposite page:
Jacqueline-face
Bride, 21 inches,
vinyl, 1965

Right: Wendy Brides, from left: 1991-92; 1993-94; 1995; 1966-90; each 8 inches, hard plastic

Below: Elises, from left: Bride, 1960; Bride, 1958; Pink Bride, 1959; each 17 inches, hard plastic and vinyl

Opposite page, top: Bride, 21 inches, porcelain, 1989-90; limited edition of 2,500

Opposite page, bottom: Cissys, from left: Bride, 1962; Bridesmaid, 1958; Bride, 1958; each 21 inches, hard plastic and vinyl

Celebrations and Traditions

Madame Alexander's very first commercial success in the 1920s was the creation of a doll depicting a Red Cross nurse. She knew that the image saluting the brave women who had so recently risked their lives in World War I would be popular with children and their parents. Since that first success, the Alexander Doll Company has continued to make dolls that honor the meaningful aspects of our lives. From the diminutive composition Birthday Dolls of 1937 to today's cheerful Rice Krispies™ characters that recall family breakfasts for millions of Americans, there are always dolls in the company's collection that celebrate daily life and its many traditions.

While continuing to honor American values with dolls like the United States Armed Forces collection, the Alexander Doll Company upholds Madame's pledge to educate through her dolls by paying homage to the variety of world cultures through her International Dolls, and through those that celebrate the world's many holidays.

Below: U. S. Armed Forces, from left: U. S. Air Force; U.S. Marine; U.S. Navy; U.S. Army; each 8 inches inches, hard plastic, 1997
Opposite page: Chinese New Year set with dragon, from left: Sue Li; Lei Li; Ming Li; each 8 inches, hard plastic, 1995

Birthday Dolls, from left: January; April; February; June;
May; March; each 7 inches, composition, 1937-39

International Dolls, front row, from left: India, 1965-84; Dutch Girl, 1961-91, Dutch Boy, 1964-
89; Vietnam, 1968-69; center row, from left: Bolivia, 1963-66; Israel, 1965-88; Russia, 1965-84;
Japan, 1968-90; China, 1972-89; Argentina, 1965-86; back row, from left: Africa, 1966-71;
Australia, 1990-91; Scotland, 1961-91; Tunisia, 1989; Indonesia, 1970-88;
Poland, 1964-88; Ecuador, 1963-66; Spain, 1961-85; each 8 inches, hard plastic

International Dolls, front row, from left: Egypt, 1986-89; Panama, 1985-87; Mali, 1996-97; Chile, 1992; Cossack, 1989-91; Philippines, 1987; back row, from left: Peruvian Boy, 1965-66; Morocco, 1968-70; Lapland, 1993; Thailand, 1966-89; Jamaica, 1986-88; Tyrolean Boy & Girl, 1962-86; each 8 inches, hard plastic

Birthday Dolls, from left: July; September; October; November; August; December; each 7 inches, composition, 1937-39

Above: International Dolls, from left: Egypt, 1998; Mexico, 1997; England, 1997; Puerto Rico, 1998; France, 1996-99; United States of America, 1996-99; Ireland, 1996-99; Italy, 1997; each 8 inches, hard plastic

Right: Happy Chanukah, 8 inches, hard plastic, 1995

Opposite page: International Dolls, from left: India, 1965-84; Vietnam, 1968-69; each 8 inches, hard plastic

Above: The Nativity, music box crêche with, clockwise from Wise Man in gold: Shepherd; Mary; Angel; Baby Jesus in manger; Joseph; Drummer Boy; Wise Men; each 8 inches, hard plastic, 1997

Left, from left: Santa's Little Helper; Christmas Holly; each 8 inches, hard plastic, 1998

Below: Zodiac Collection, top photo, from left: Capricorn, 1997; Aquarius, 1997; Pisces, 1997; Aries, 1997; Taurus, 1998; Gemini, 1998; each 8 inches, hard plastic; bottom photo, from left: Cancer; Leo; Virgo; Libra; Scorpio; Sagittarius; each 8 inches, hard plastic, 1998

Opposite page:
Watchful Guardian
Angel, 10 inches;
Forrest, 8 inches;
Heather, 8 inches;
each hard plastic,
1998

Above, from left:
Cupid—The
Messenger of Love,
8 inches, hard plas-
tic, 1997; Guardian
Angel, 1997; Pink
Pristine Angel, 1997;
Glistening Angel
Treetopper, 1998;
each 10 inches,
hard plastic

Left: Rice Krispies™
from left: Crackle,™
Snap,™ and Pop,™
each 8 inches,
hard plastic, 1998

Part 3

How the Dolls are Made

From Conception to Creation

In New York City, in an uptown Manhattan neighborhood known as Harlem, there lies a portal to enchantment. From the exterior, the building in question is a plain-looking structure. Slightly nondescript and strictly utilitarian, the edifice once housed the Studebaker automobile plant, a manufacturer that blissfully billed itself in the 1930s as a "purveyor of automotive dreams." Today, the West 131st Street address is the headquarters of the Alexander Doll Company. Inside this urban complex are brightly painted pink-and-blue halls and walls, and within the office suites and on the factory floors work the talented men and women who strive daily to keep Madame Beatrice Alexander's dollmaking dreams alive.

Below: One of the company's senior designers, John Puzewski, begins the process of creating a new doll by sketching his ideas. Opposite page: Draping a doll with sample fabric is the first step in making a three-dimensional rendering of a new concept.

The Alexander Doll Company's motto today is "Love is in the details." Those who work there look toward Madame Alexander each and every day for inspiration. Madame's presence is felt as employees walk through the halls, search through the archives, or talk with people who know the company's history. Madame's goal that "dolls are to be loved" is pursued daily. As a possible good-luck totem, and a connection to past achievements, the original doors that once swung open to Madame's showroom in The Toy Center on Fifth Avenue now hang decoratively at the entrance to the factory floor.

A doll that is created by the Alexander Doll Company enters this world as an heir to Madame's perfectionism and idealism. An Alexander doll is a manufactured product that receives hands-on attention and meticulous personalized inspection every step of the way. The quality control that is demanded from one procedure to the next is a testament to how seriously the Alexander craftsmen and women view their jobs.

How, then, does a freckle-faced Maggie Mix-Up or a beauty-marked Cissette come to show-

Above: Creation of the sample doll
involves many talents and many hands.
Above right: Designer Marianne Graf
compares trims and fabrics to original reference materials. Right: Senior designer
Daun Fallon examines a sample.

case such vastly different appearances? Why do certain Wendy-faced dolls end up as cheerleaders and fire fighters, while others become Shakespearean heroines and nursery-rhyme heroes? A doll's journey from imagination to reality occurs under the roof of this Manhattan manufacturing plant, where dreams have seemingly always had a home. And the doll's voyage from conception to creation is a fascinating path to follow.

The Alexander Doll Company employs approximately five hundred people; four hundred in the factory and one hundred in administrative capacities. Counted among the latter are the firm's eight design-

Right and below: A hairstyle is created on the sample doll and then eyelashes are carefully painted. Opposite page: A reference board showcases the wide variety of shoe styles from which the designers select the perfect footwear for their new creation.

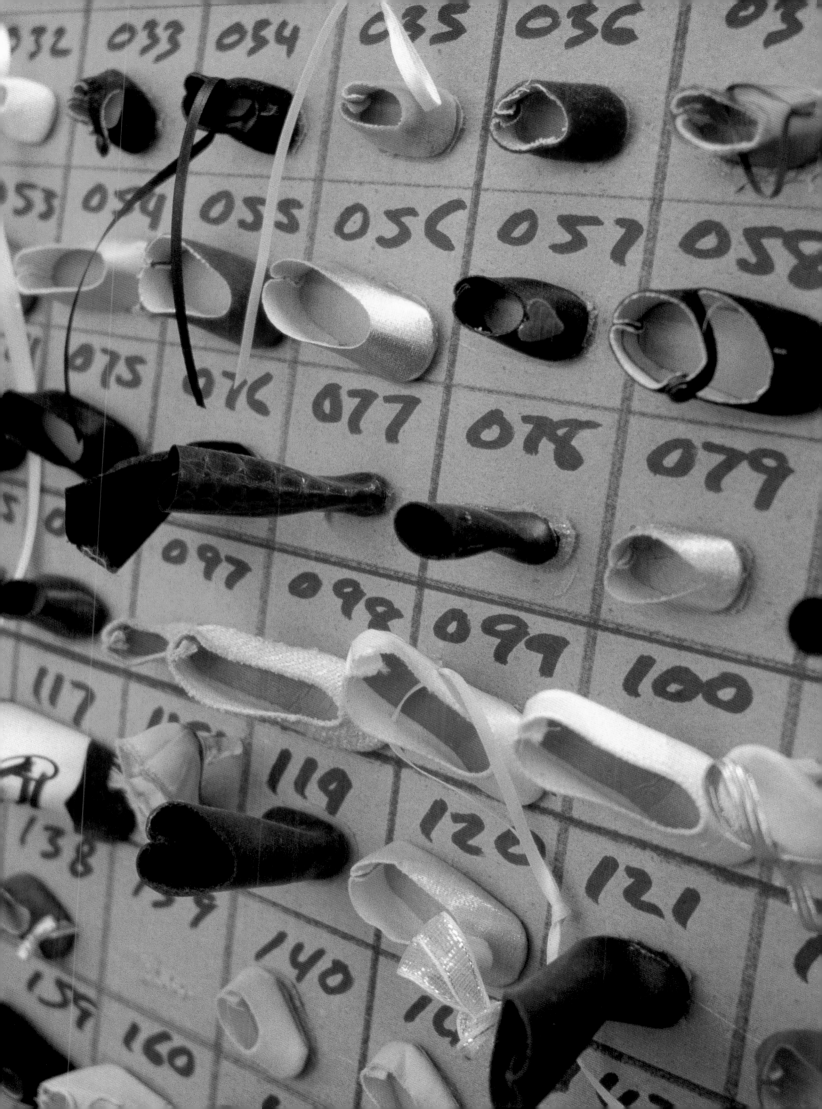

Above: Senior designer Daun Fallon reviews pre-production samples.
Right: A variety of metal face-painting stencils are used to create perfect lips and eyebrows.
Opposite page: This exotic-looking stencil is used for painting eyebrows.

ers. Periodically, the company hosts brainstorming meetings where the designers and various department executives gather together and discuss ideas to pursue for future dolls. When a concept is enthusiastically approved, the designers break up into teams and begin to flesh out the suggestions. Designers may surround themselves with volumes of historical research, if the suggested costuming is from a past time period. Or they might immerse themselves in a book on ballet or

an artist's masterpiece oil painting, if the proposed doll is a tribute to one of the fine arts. Some of the designers sketch their ideas in detail, presenting a final two-dimensional rendering for the next viewing. Others design by draping fabric directly onto a doll's body, and present their concept as a three-dimensional rendering.

Everyone who attends contributes his or her viewpoints to this very important decision process. The length of hair; the shade of eyebrows;

Opposite page: Each face is carefully inspected prior to painting. Left: The first step is spray painting the lips.
Below: Blush is applied without a stencil to achieve a natural look.
Bottom: A head awaits further beautifying.

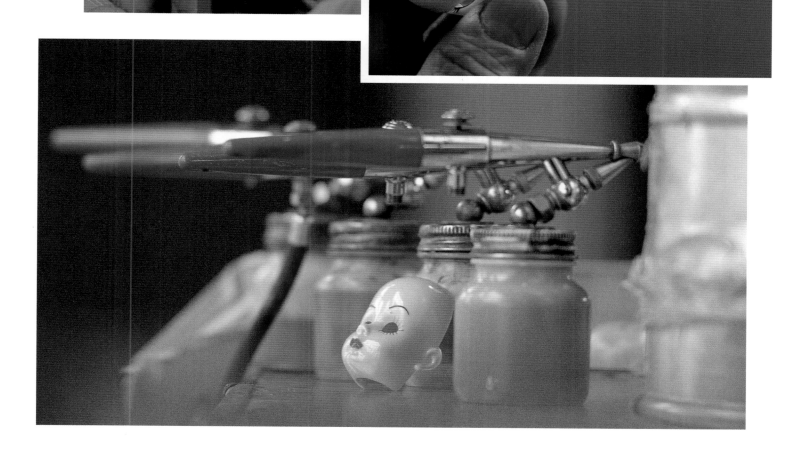

Above: Long strips of hair are wet down in preparation for curling. Above left: A hairpiece, now soft and pliable, is applied to the doll's head. Left: Once the hairpiece is secured, the hairstylist goes to work. In this case, she is creating ponytails.

whether a Margaret face or a Kelly face or a Wendy face works best; even the style of shoelace is actively discussed and then mutually approved. When a concept has passed final review, it is brought to three-dimensional life as a prototype: a one-of-a-kind doll is created by the designer and one of the firm's talented artisans. These nimble-fingered men and women work closely with the designer, who has already created a sample of the doll in its approved costume. Together, the team creates the final model from which all the dolls will be produced. At this stage, it is essential that any complaints, suggestions or reservations be voiced. Like a corporate version of the oft-quoted wedding-day nuptials, it is definitely: "Speak now, or forever hold your peace."

When a new version of one of the Little Women, or an up-to-date retooling of a Dionne Quintuplet, is given the thumbs-up, the doll is ready to be made *en masse*. The bodies and the

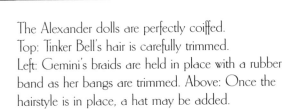

The Alexander dolls are perfectly coiffed.
Top: Tinker Bell's hair is carefully trimmed.
Left: Gemini's braids are held in place with a rubber band as her bangs are trimmed. Above: Once the hairstyle is in place, a hat may be added.

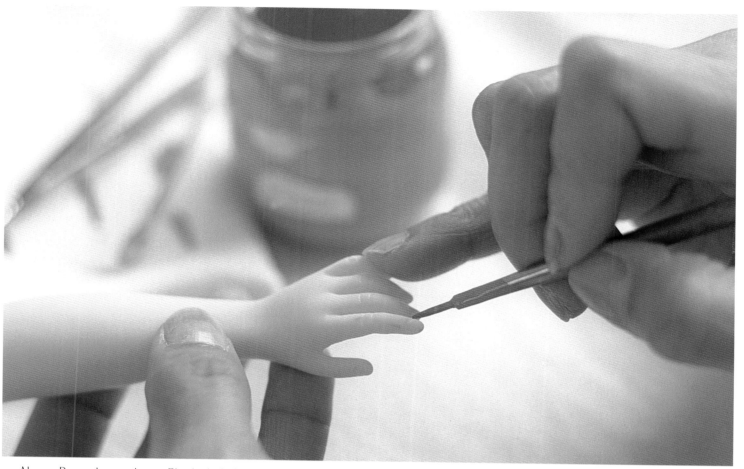

Above: Better than a day at Elizabeth Arden: an Alexander doll has her nails painted.
Right: Cutting dies in every style are used for creating the costumes. Below: An employee transports fabric for cutting.

⚜

heads of the dolls are produced from molds in a company-owned factory situated in the Bronx, then shipped to the main facility, where the crew of four hundred professionals transforms these bare, bald, expressionless parts into dolls that soon will be loved and admired.

The Alexander dolls all begin their lives as unnamed faces with indistinct components. Then, the dolls' colorful personalities come to fruition through the painting, wigging, dressing and styling processes.

Because the company has been producing dolls for more than seventy-five years, it has a veritable archive of past doll successes to draw upon. Reference numbers to popular clothing patterns and "well-worn" shoe styles are posted in the various work arenas. A designer can select a type of footwear that worked

The Doll Hospital

Greta Schrader, below, and Cosme Santiago, right, are experts in tending to the Alexander dolls that have been loved too intensely for long periods of time. From restringing loose bodies to restyling tangled hairpieces and spiffing up tired wardrobes, the men and women of the Alexander Doll Hospital minister to a well-loved doll's every need.

PHOTO: SARA MATTHEWS

well in the past, quote the already assigned number, and a new descendant of that shoe will be cobbled and stitched for a new doll to wear. Also, because so many dolls are being made on any given day—dolls from next year's line, as well as this year's and even the year before—the reference numbers of the various components help the craftspeople keep track of which figure they are drafting. During the course of a year, more than 750,000 dolls are primped, posed and packed at the Alexander plant. That translates into more than 3,000 dolls per business day! No wonder handy reference numbers and templates are tacked up wherever they are needed.

The work flow at the Alexander factory can be described as quick yet qualified. Each step of the

On the sewing floor, a staff of seamstresses creates the dolls' wardrobes, down to affixing the tiny snaps by which the clothes are fastened.

Many of the dolls' accessories are made at the factory. Above: A straw hat is sewn. Left: A worker carefully places the inner sole on the shoe. Below: The tiny shoelaces are threaded into the shoe. Opposite page: A pencil eraser proves the best tool for cleaning dolls' faces.

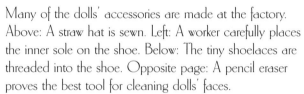

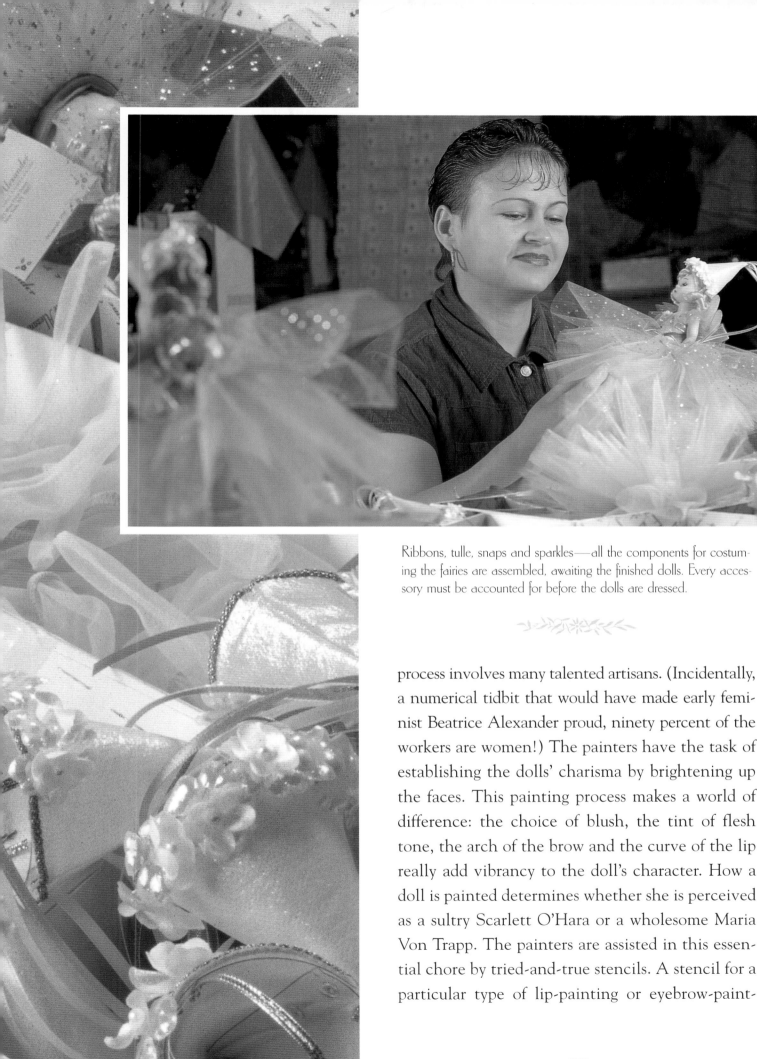

Ribbons, tulle, snaps and sparkles—all the components for costuming the fairies are assembled, awaiting the finished dolls. Every accessory must be accounted for before the dolls are dressed.

process involves many talented artisans. (Incidentally, a numerical tidbit that would have made early feminist Beatrice Alexander proud, ninety percent of the workers are women!) The painters have the task of establishing the dolls' charisma by brightening up the faces. This painting process makes a world of difference: the choice of blush, the tint of flesh tone, the arch of the brow and the curve of the lip really add vibrancy to the doll's character. How a doll is painted determines whether she is perceived as a sultry Scarlett O'Hara or a wholesome Maria Von Trapp. The painters are assisted in this essential chore by tried-and-true stencils. A stencil for a particular type of lip-painting or eyebrow-paint-

Above: Amy from the Little Women Journals™ set is carefully primped by her dresser, who ties a perfect bow, right, and affixes the 75th-anniversary hang tag, opposite page.

ing is held up to the doll's face and the paint is sprayed through the chosen stencil. Voilà! Cissy's knowing glance and Marybel's sleepy bedtime demeanor can be captured perfectly again and again and again. Each painted face is inspected for any mishaps or errors, no matter how seemingly minute.

After a doll's face is painted to perfection, it is further modified by the addition of its hairpiece. Many of the wigs are made by hand at the factory,

and they significantly contribute to the difference between a childlike doll, such as Fire Fighter Wendy, and an elegantly garbed Diamond Beauty. The material for the hair comes in long synthetic strips that a worker wets down and then places on a long curling iron. The hair is baked for eight hours, and when the timing is completed, the strip of hair has a lifelike permanent wave. The hair strips are cut to size, and the end result is softness and pliability. The Alexander hairpieces behave in a very lifelike manner, and the color choices of blond, brunette and auburn were selected to mirror real people's pigmentations. Except, of course, when a fantastically coiffed *Alice in Wonderland* or *Wizard of Oz*™ character has to be designed—then the rainbowed-sky becomes the limit for dyeing and tinting and crimping.

Correspondingly, the wardrobe that distinguishes an Alexander doll is often based upon what real-live men and women wear. The four Fashion Academy Gold Medals that Madame won in the 1950s attested to her desire to treat her miniature models as *haute-couture* surrogates, and today's Alexander designers often follow that same diminutive-diva theme. The outfits that the pattern-makers and the seamstresses create at the factory would not be out of place in a Seventh Avenue atelier. Millinery magic, neckline jeweling and bodice beading are all done by hand as part of an Alexander workday. The seamstresses and garment workers who produce the fashions for Cissy, Elise and the newest porcelain launch, Catherine, are as committed to quality as Calvin Klein's or Donna Karan's die-cutters and sewing circle. The term "manufacture" often conjures up—mistakenly—an Orwellian image of disembodied, robotic drones and ceaseless steel convey-

accountable not only to herself, but to her co-workers, as well. That is why the Alexander dolls are handled and inspected and cared for so thoroughly and so sincerely during their travels from procedure to procedure.

The final stop in the factory is the dressing department where the dolls are matched up with their detailed finery. Depending upon whether it is about to begin life as a Southern belle or as a brave Armed Forces soldier, at this stop each doll is either snugly laced into hand-embroidered undergarments or crisply suited-up in authentic military dress. The dedicated men and women who make up these teams are expected to affix the wigs, button-up or snap-down each outfit, and account for all the accessories. Additionally, they run the final, thorough examination of every hosiery seam, and ensure that every cheek is unblemished and clean. The workers in this department place the approved dolls into the world-famous pink-and-blue boxes, and tuck them into a bed of crisp pink tissue paper. After a day of beauty far more thorough than anything ever promised at Elizabeth Arden, these Alexander creations are shipped to doll shops and collectors around the world, as the Alexander Doll Company strives daily to honor its past and create beloved dolls for the future..

or belts. At Alexander, the term more accurately refers to a team-based approach that ensures a continuous-flow process and high-quality production.

One of the most essential reasons the Alexander Doll Company is able to create three-quarters of a million dolls per year is the Kaizen work ethic, a Japanese-based approach in which each worker is taught to respect what he or she is doing. A seamstress who attaches bows to pantaloons or who stitches rosettes to bonnets is instructed to view each and every finished garment as something she has created and now *owns*. Everyone who works within a group and within a department is responsible for what emerges from that work station, and therefore each worker is

Part 4

Collectors' Information